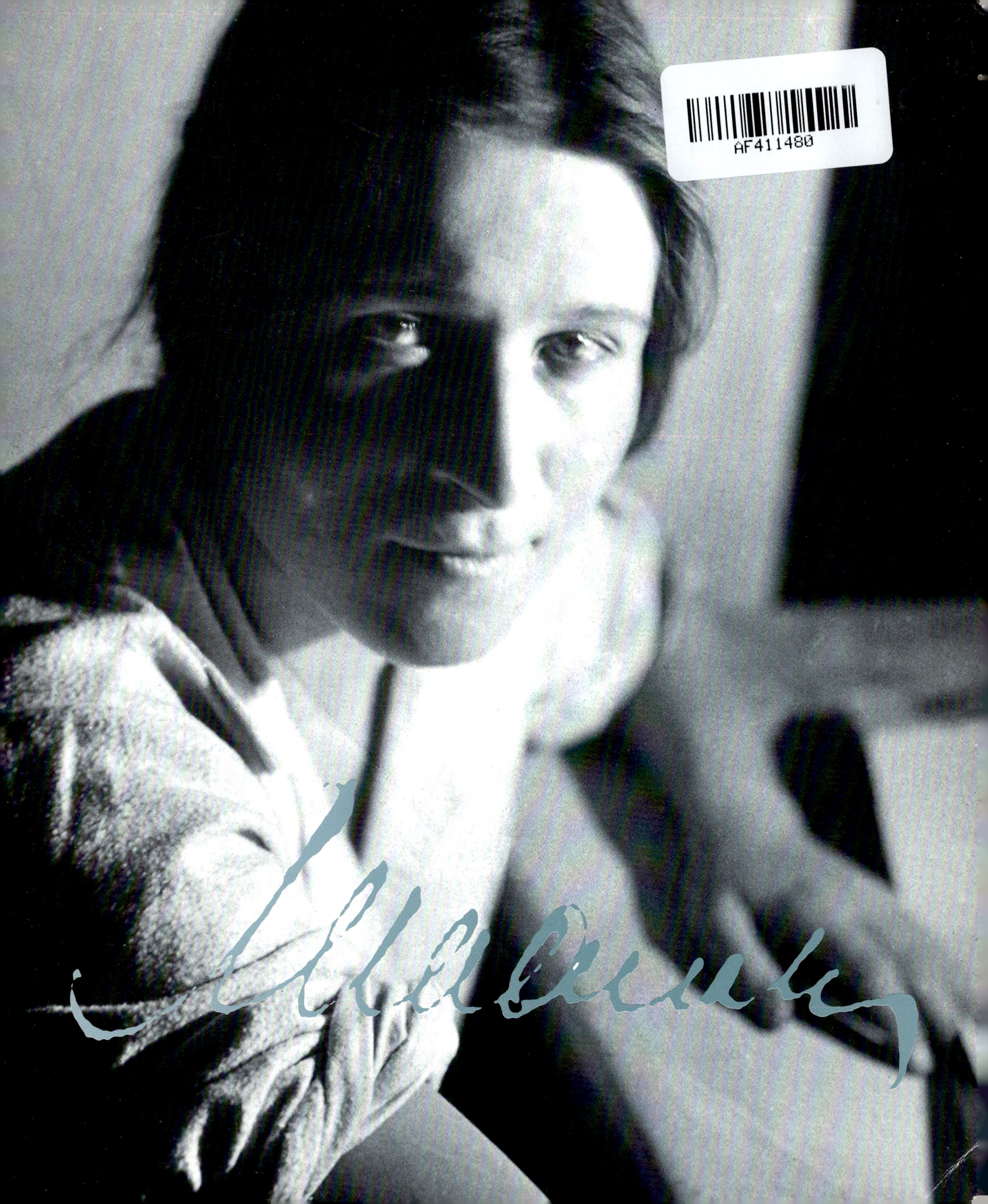
AF411480

Myriad Thoughts, Myriad Desires:

LIUDMILA IVANOVA

(1904–1977)

An Artist in Soviet Russia

Fisher Gallery, University of Southern California
March 15–April 22, 2000

Myriad Thoughts, Myriad Desires:

LIUDMILA IVANOVA

(1904–1977)

An Artist in Soviet Russia

FACULTY CURATORS
JOHN E. BOWLT
NICOLETTA MISLER

CURATORS
RANDI HOKETT
RIKA IEZUMI
RAIMOND LIVASGANI
WALTER MEYER
LINDA M. OH
ROMY M. VREELAND

TECHNICAL EDITORS
JOHN E. BOWLT
PETER SCHERTZ

EXHIBITION COORDINATOR
JENNIFER JASKOWIAK

*A collaboration with
USC Department of Slavic
Languages and Literature
and Institute of Modern
Russian Culture*

© 2000 Fisher Gallery, University of Southern California
823 Exposition Boulevard
University Park
Los Angeles, CA 90089-0292
ISBN: 0-9451922-4-X
Library of Congress Catalog Card Number: 99-68251

All rights reserved. No part of this catalog may be
reproduced in any form by electronic means, including
information storage and retrieval systems, without
permission in writing from the USC Fisher Gallery except
by a reviewer who may quote brief passages in review.

DESIGN AND PRODUCTION
Sibylle Hagmann, *Graphic Designer, USC School of Architecture*
Sarah Lovett, *Design Assistant*
Randi Hokett, *USC Museum Studies Program*

COPY EDITOR
Linda M. Oh, *USC Museum Studies Program*

PRINTER
Typecraft, Inc. Pasadena

USC FISHER GALLERY STAFF
Selma Holo, *Director*
Kay Allen, *Associate Director*
Jennifer Jaskowiak, *Curator/Exhibitions Coordinator*
Max F. Schulz, *Curator of Exhibitions*
Jeanette C. LaVere, *Education and Outreach Coordinator*
Brian Olson, *Preparator and Exhibition Designer*
Matt Driggs, *Gallery Security/Preparator's Assistant*
Kevin Parker, *Administrative Assistant*
Ariadni Liokatis, *Curatorial Intern*

PHOTO CREDITS
Unless otherwise indicated, images are reproduced with
permission of the Institute of Modern Russian Culture,
University of Southern California.

ON THE FLY
Luidmila Ivanova (G15) c. 1920s

Table of Contents

Acknowledgements

Many individuals and institutions contributed to the materialization of "Myriad Thoughts, Myriad Desires." Throughout, the unwavering moral support of our family and friends fueled our excitement, enthusiasm and dedication during trials and tribulations. This exhibition is as much theirs as ours.

Special thanks go to Felix Ravdonikas. His courageous act to save his mother's oeuvre under perilous circumstances and his subsequent gift of these works to the IMRC ensures access to an important portion of history, Russian Modernism. Further, we are indebted to conservators Linda Shaffer and Aneta Zebala; we are genuinely in awe of their steadfast dedication to the conservation of art.

Ineffable gratitude is extended to John E. Bowlt and Nicoletta Misler. This exhibition is their brainchild. They are wonderful role models who afforded us their scholarly expertise as well as many moments of enlightenment, humor and afternoon tea. They helped us cross the disciplinary bridge and create a truly multidimensional project.

We offer exceptional thanks to Selma Holo and Jennifer Jaskowiak, respectively, the director and curator of USC Fisher Gallery, who have been the true North on our compass, and to the entire Fisher Gallery staff for helping us navigate gracefully the intricate process of the exhibition organization.

We are much indebted to Sibylle Hagmann, for echoing the thematic visual coherence of our ideas into a visually sound and attractive catalog; Christa Kotrouzinis of Galerie Gmurzynska in Cologne, Germany, Mark Konecny, Karen Myers, and Sarah Pratt for their advice and encouragement; Mike Bonnet, for his photography skills; Peter Schertz for his keen eye and skillful editorial hand; and Erica Clark for advising us at the initial stages of our development campaign.

We extend our thanks to those whose assistance was motivated by friendship and the spirit of altruistic support: Dr. Lloyd Armstrong Jr., University Provost, and Dr. Morton O. Schapiro, Dean of the College of Letters, Arts, and Sciences, the faculty of the Department of Art History in the College, and its chair, Nancy Troy.

Finally, we would like to acknowledge the generous support of the Ahmanson Humanities Initiative in the College of Letters, Arts, and Sciences and the Graduate Professional Student Senate at USC (conservation, education, and publications); Ms. Juliet Der Avanessian (conservation); and Mr. and Mrs. Ronald and Roxolanna Meyer (conservation). In this legion of patrons we are especially thankful to Aneta Zebala who voluntarily conserved 16 additional paintings, the cost of which was beyond our budget, and to Cheryl Richardson for affording us a magnificent reception by volunteering her services as a liaison between Shutters on the Beach and the USC Museum Studies Program.

Notes to the Reader

Transliteration

The transliteration in this catalog modifies the Library of Congress system, either omitting the Russian soft and hard signs or rendering them by an "i" (e.g., Grigoriev). This system is also used for references to Russian language sources in the footnotes and the bibliographical data. "Myriad Thoughts, Myriad Desires: Liudmila Ivanova (1904-1977), An Artist in Soviet Russia" will be seen and read by people who appreciate the visual arts, but who may not know Russian. Consequently, we have avoided the more sophisticated transliteration systems that, to the layperson, may render a common name unrecognizable and we have retained the English-language equivalents of the names Aleksandr (Alexander), Aleksei (Alexis), and Feliks (Felix) throughout.

Times and Places

Dates referring to events in Russia before January, 1918 are twelve days behind the Western calendar if they are in the nineteenth century and thirteen days behind if they are between 1900 and 1918.

The city of St. Petersburg was renamed Petrograd in 1914, Leningrad in 1924, and then St. Petersburg again in 1992. However, both the names Petrograd and St. Petersburg continued to be used freely in common parlance and in publications until 1924. As a general rule, however, Petrograd has been retained here as the official name of St. Petersburg for the period 1914-1924.

Frequently mentioned institutions and organizations have been abbreviated in text and notes. Please see the Glossary of Terms and Acronyms.

Sources

The paintings, drawings, and documents in "Myriad Thoughts, Myriad Desires" come from the Liudmila Ivanova bequest held by the Institute of Modern Russian Culture at the University of Southern California, Los Angeles. Because of space limitations and the fragility of some works, this exhibition includes only part of the corpus. However, the entire collection has been inventoried by alphabetical category and number and the assigned inventory number is provided each time a painting, drawing, or document is mentioned (e.g. G14).

Foreword

SELMA HOLO

It is my pleasure to introduce "Myriad Thoughts, Myriad Desires: Liudmila Ivanova (1904-1977), An Artist in Soviet Russia," an exhibition curated by the University of Southern California's Museum Studies Program under the supervision of Professors John Bowlt and Nicoletta Misler. Professor Bowlt and I have wanted to research and mount at Fisher Gallery of the University of Southern California an exhibition of Ivanova's work for many years; "Myriad Thoughts, Myriad Desires" became the perfect vehicle for fulfilling that desire while working with our own students.

Our students in the Museum Studies Program at USC earn a Master's degree in art history with a specialization in museum studies; every exhibition they curate in that program stands on a firm foundation of art historical studies. In the case of the Ivanova exhibition, Professor Bowlt led a seminar in the spring of 1999 in which the Museum Studies students as well as his doctoral students in Russian studies participated. These students had the excitement of working with original, almost completely unknown material replete with the cultural, political, and artistic issues of the period and place of its creation. The challenges posed by the material were compounded by the physical delicacy of the objects themselves. In the tears, creases, foxing, and dirt that have marked these drawings and paintings can be seen all the residue of this momentous century. Thus, in mounting this exhibition, our students have had to struggle not only with issues of installation, but also fundamental issues of art history and conservation.

This catalog is the lasting evidence of the scholarly work that our students have done on this unique early twentieth-century Russian woman artist who has never before been featured in a museum exhibition. While doing honor and justice to Ivanova, this catalog also exemplifies the students' and the Fisher Gallery's commitment to present their scholarship in a way that speaks to specialists and generalists. I want to acknowledge the hard work of each and every student and the excellence of their product. I also wish to thank Professors John Bolwt and Nicoletta Misler for their sustained involvement in the project. I wish to thank Fisher Gallery's Curator, Jennifer Jaskowiak, for her supervision of the museum studies students in every single stage of the exhibition—from the proverbial soup to nuts! I thank the entire staff of USC's Fisher Gallery for their work with the students and Peter Schertz for his fine editing of their essays. I also wish to thank Nancy Troy, Chair of the Art History Department and the College of Letters, Arts and Sciences for their ongoing support.

Congratulations are in order to the members of the Ivanova team for the excellent exhibition they have wrought!

Selma Holo, Ph.D.
Director
Museum Studies Program, Department of Art History

Preface:
Myriad Thoughts, Myriad Desires

JOHN E. BOWLT

The exhibition "Myriad Thoughts, Myriad Desires: Liudmila Ivanova (1904-1977), An Artist in Soviet Russia" and its catalog are the fruit of a close and vital collaboration between many forces, interdisciplinary and interdepartmental—museological, art historical, and linguistic— at the University of Southern California, Los Angeles. The very diversity of these forces served us in good stead, because, from the outset, our team was forced to address and resolve many difficult and disparate questions: How, for example, to assess and present an artist whose work lacked critical acclaim, an artist whose curriculum vitae contained serious lacunae and inconsistencies, an artist who never contributed to professional exhibitions, an artist who belonged to a foreign culture and an alien regime, an artist whose *œuvre* was full of stylistic contradictions? Not surprisingly, therefore, during its gestation and evolution our venture underwent many changes as did our critical approach to the fundamental issues of inventorying, catalog design, selecting works, conservation, restoration, and installation— issues that demanded keen energy and initiative as well as an unfailing dedication to the project.

For all our commitment and passion, "Myriad Thoughts, Myriad Desires" would not have been possible without the transfer of the Ivanova estate to the Institute of Modern Russian Culture at the University of Southern California in 1989 and the earnest encouragement of the exhibition by her family in Russia and Germany. Thanks both to this complex bequest of paintings, drawings, photographs, and documents and, in particular, to the eager support of Felix Ravdonikas, Ivanova's son, we were able to envision and prepare such an ambitious survey of her work in an accredited museum and with a professional catalog. True, immediately after the accession of the collection, Karen Myers, a specialist in Russian Modernism, curated "The Knowing Eye," a small exhibition of selected paintings and drawings from the estate at the IMRC in 1990; that was, as the Russians say, the *pervaia lastochka* ["first swallow"], and it immediately became clear that the quality, quantity, and diversity of Ivanova's *œuvre* dictated a major retrospective in a major exhibiting institution. Fortunately, the innovative structure of the Museum Studies Program at the University of Southern California enabled us to establish a graduate seminar devoted to Ivanova and the Russian avant-garde, to assess and register all the works in the collection, to have select pieces cleaned and restored, to prepare the exhibition, and to compile and, then, publish this catalog.

"Myriad Thoughts, Myriad Desires" is an archaeological expedition into the rich substratum of Russian Modernism, a metaphor that may have appealed to Ivanova's own ethnographic and anthropological orientation in the 1930s. The artifacts that grace the surface of the Russian avant-garde are common currency—the lyrical abstraction of Vasilii Kandinsky, the Suprematism of Kazimir Malevich, the photography of Alexander Rodchenko, and the reliefs of Vladimir Tatlin are the subjects of universal acceptance and veneration; but the brilliance of these inventions has blinded us to the accomplishments of many other Russian artists and writers of the 1910s and 1920s, especially of the second generation of the avant-garde after the October Revolution. Moscow, too, has tended to occupy the primary attention of historians, although it is becoming increasingly clear that St. Petersburg/Leningrad, Kharkov, Kiev, Odessa, Saratov, and Smolensk (not to mention Vitebsk) played crucial roles in the adaptation and dissemination of radical artistic ideas in the 1910s and 1920s.

Ivanova was a part of that margin and of that generation fascinated by the radical ideas of her most compelling mentors, Pavel Filonov, Mikhail Matiushin, and Kuzma Petrov-Vodkin; yet, she was mindful of the new social and political demands made upon culture as pressures for a more narrative emphasis came to replace the brave experiments of the avant-garde. Never a Socialist Realist as it was defined and promoted in the Stalinist era, Ivanova painted unpretentious subjects (the simple Russian landscape, the colors of spring and autumn) in a style that had none of the false rhetoric and bombast associated with the grand gestures of Stalin's court painters. In this sense, Ivanova, like many other artists of her time, steered an artistic course that, for all its modesty and serenity, was fraught with danger, simply because it avoided the prescribed themes of industrial transformation, agricultural abundance, and glorification of the leader.

But assessment of Ivanova's work tells us not only about the evolution and survival of an artist during the time of terror, but also, perhaps paradoxically, about her genuine support of the Soviet regime—and about the tragic paradoxes of this position. A person of warmth and sincerity, Ivanova became a member of the Communist Party of the Soviet Union in 1939—just two years after experiencing the cruelty of the Secret Police with the arrest of her second husband and removal of her second son to a foster home. Nurtured by the avant-garde, especially Filonov, she seems to have experienced inner freedom only when she broke with her teachers and rediscovered realism; living most of her life in the Neo-Classical splendor of the "Venice of the North," she found her greatest artistic satisfaction in the hills, lakes, and churches of the countryside—even if these gentle landscapes seem still pervaded by the disturbing light of the Aurora Borealis and the White Nights of St. Petersburg; marked by the tribulations and trials of three marriages and five children, she defended the role of the exemplary Soviet wife and mother; introspective and of mercurial temperament (as her private diaries and correspondence reveal), Ivanova supported the social and cultural institutions that controlled public ritual during the conformist decades of the 1930s and 1940s.

Ivanova was a painter, designer, teacher, wife, mother, and political champion. Registering Ivanova's achievements in life and art and her encounters with the countless practical and ideological problems of her time (the stifling bureaucracy, the need to conform, the lack of basic supplies, the immobility of public institutions, the Party's omnipresence, the censure of digression) has helped us to understand more clearly the predicament of the average

Soviet citizen during Stalin's reign. These issues as well as the complex pattern of Ivanova's artistic career itself have informed, if not generated, the wide diapason of essays in this catalog—on the avant-garde, on language, on museological reception, on the ethics of restoration, and on Soviet Russia. Above all, researching the life and work of Liudmila Ivanova, coaxing an unfamiliar artist into the pantheon of Russian culture, composing the exhibition, and writing the catalog have confronted us with the most basic issues of æsthetic appreciation, with the uneasy conventions of the academy and market-place, and—*horribile dictu*—with the monstrous foibles and divisive prejudices that fashion and dictate the assumptions and conventions of art history itself.

John E. Bowlt

Liudmila Alexandrovna Ivanova
Biographical Scheme

Fig. 1 Ivanova's Matrikula (G14) 1926

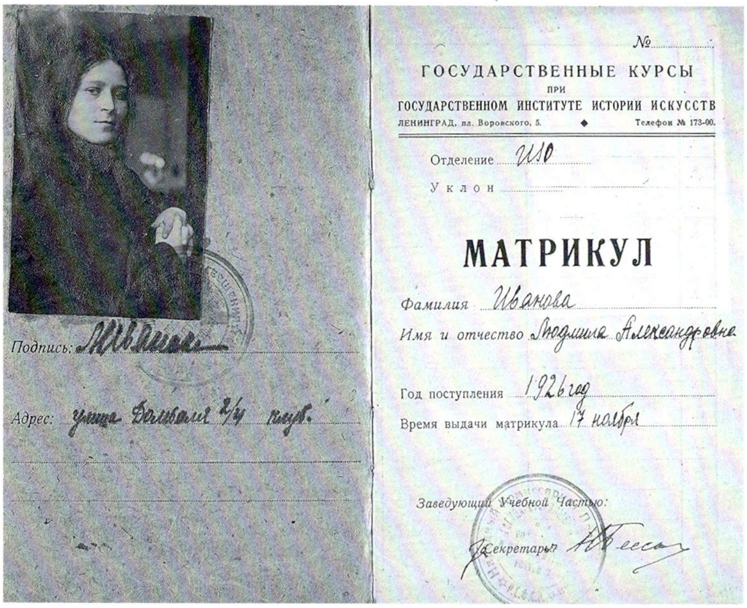

1904 Born 27 August (9 September).
Liudmila Ivanova's family was of mixed social and cultural background. Her father, Alexander Ivanovich (1879-1927), was a locomotive driver and then a highly qualified metalworker at a St. Petersburg factory and a close friend of Mikhail Kalinin—later the chairman of the Bolshevik Parliament under Lenin and then Stalin. Ivanova's mother, Lidiia Efremova (née Arkhangelskaia, 1881-1931), was a couturier, whose clients included ladies of high station. In this way and from an early age, Liudmila Ivanova was exposed both to the cult of the industrial machine and to closed ideological systems as well as to the world of haute couture and the applied arts.

1915 Enrolls in the Vladimir Society Trade School after attending primary school.

1918 Transfers to the Soviet United Labor School (formerly the Marina Women's Gymnasium).

1920-1922 Attends the School for the Encouragement of the Arts.

1921 Enrolls in the Academy of Arts as a sponsee of the Metal Workers Labor Union and Regional Committee of the Komsomol. The academy's faculty includes leading representatives of Russian Modernism, including Altman, Matiushin, Petrov-Vodkin, and Tatlin; Ivanova studies under Matiushin and, presumably, Petrov-Vodkin.

1922 Father deserts the family; parents divorce.

1923 Marries Ignatii Tatarovich; candidate for membership in the Communist Party (possibly 1924); member of the Komsomol.

1924 Birth of first son, Vladimir; mother diagnosed with cancer; candidate for membership in the Communist Party. Contact with Filonov's group of students who became known as the Collective of Masters of Analytical Art in 1925.

1926 Romance with fellow-student Nikolai Kuranov; divorces Tatarovich; diagnosed with tuberculosis; graduates from the Academy on 11 September; enrolls in the

Higher State Art-Historical Courses (State Institute of Art History).

1926-1927 Works at the City Museum copying antique maps of Peterhof and other palatial complexes.

1927 Father dies of alcohol poisoning.

1927-1928 Assistant curator at the Leningrad State Museum Fund.

1928-1930 Research assistant at the State Russian Museum.

Late 1920s Close to Filonov; designs cigarette packages for a Leningrad tobacco factory.

1930 Marries Kuranov (one source dates this marriage to 1927).

1930-1931 Works as a designer for the Leningrad Visual Arts Publishing House.

1931 Mother dies; birth of second son, Yurii; works with the Collective of Masters of Analytical Art on illustrations for a Russian translation of the Finnish epos *Kalevala* (published by Academia, Leningrad, in 1933).

1931-1933 Enrolls in the graduate program of the Hermitage; member of design team for the exhibitions "Caricatures during the Great French Revolution" and "Pre-Class Society during the Sarmathian-Goth Period."

1933-1934 Research assistant at AIMK where she meets Vladislav Ravdonikas.

1934 Divorces Kuranov (one source gives 1936 as year of divorce), leaving Yurii with him; marries her third husband, the historian and ethnographer, Vladislav Ravdonikas; in the fall, experiences an artistic crisis, breaking away from the Filonov school to pursue a more Realist style, although retains her veneration of Filonov himself.

1934-1935 Political editor and reader for the newspaper *Leningradskaia Pravda* [Leningrad Pravda], the Leningrad District City Literature Office, and the Visual Arts Section of the City literature Office; experiments with new techniques (such as linocut and etching) and materials (such as stone and linoleum).

1936 Becomes an editor and designer for the Visual Arts Publishing House, Leningrad; illustrates and designs the cover and binding for Vladislav Ravdonikas's two volume *Naskalnye izobrazheniia Onezhskogo ozera i Belogo moria* [Cliff Drawings of Onezh Lake and the White Sea] (Moscow-Leningrad: Academy of Arts of the USSR, 1936-1938).

1937 Birth of her third son (and first with Ravdonikas), Felix; Kuranov is arrested and exiled to Siberia after betrayal by Trukhachev, a fellow worker at the Hermitage and former *Filonovians*; their son, Yurii, is sent to an orphanage and for more than a decade Ivanova loses track of him.

1938 Birth of her daughter, Isabella.

1939-1977 Member of the Communist Party.

1941 Rift with Ravdonikas leads to their divorce in the spring, although they remarry in June—a day before the USSR enters the Second World War; Ivanova and her children are evacuated to the eastern part of Russia where she directs a children's home until the end of the War; Ravdonikas remains in Leningrad, surviving imprisonment, the German blockade, debilitation, and disease.

1945 Ivanova returns to Leningrad; birth of fifth child, the daughter Inna; divorces Ravdonikas.

1948 Starts to teach at the Leningrad Mukhina Higher Industrial Art Institute.

Late 1940s-1950s Teaches and works as a museum designer and installer.

1961 Retires.

1977 Dies 8 January, Leningrad; Ravdonikas dies.

My Mother, Liudmila Ivanova

FELIX RAVDONIKAS

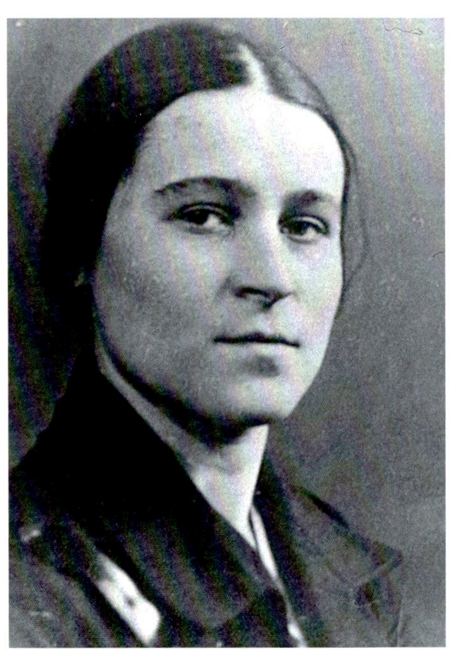

Fig. 2 Liudmila Ivanova (G8a) 1921

"I shall bend all my energy to painting. Once again I'm a human being, in all human greatness and power. I look forward to my future. Everything is clear to me now."[1] With these words, my mother, Liudmila Ivanova, concluded her diary entry for 12 September 1934, a day that marked her freedom from artistic subordination and her discovery of a new era of artistic truth.

12 September 1934: Day's end. It's the first in ten years…I was painting and the tears were rushing down my face, my hands, the easel…for the first time in years I was sorry that I had quit painting…And I was painting from the sketch that I made from inside the canyon, a view of Cherkes-Kermen in the mountains…I did everything directly with the brush. All colors have been laid down, all forms are clean cut. Light and shadow, everything is in place. Suede hills with dazzling white cliffs in the foreground…Not a single trace of infirmity, weakness, or technical retardation…I burst into tears…when I had finished the painting and worked through the sky, the expanse, the snow-white cliffs in the foreground blinded me, hiding those terrible…Filonovian mugs…With the disappearance of these terrible mugs, of this nightmare from my canvas, I feel as if heavy chains have fallen from my body. I trembled from happiness, from knowing that I had destroyed them with my own hands.[2]

The pejorative "Filonovian mugs" (the way in which Filonov's students used to refer to each other—as "Filonov cubs"— also bore bestial overtones) describes her own work, i.e., it is not the teacher, but the method, that is coming under fire.

After rejecting Filonov's Analytical Art, Ivanova never returned to it, even though she always held him in high regard. I, her son, am a primary witness to this and can affirm that, whether at home or in company, Ivanova never censured Filonov. At the same time, shortly before the official campaign mounted against Filonov began in earnest, Ivanova started work at the City Literature Office, i.e., in the institution directly responsible for controlling and eradicating ideological deviation. Documents in the Ivanova archive—i.e., the proofs of Vera Anikieva's essay for the catalog of the ill-fated Filonov exhibition in 1929—help clarify her "social acquiescence."[3] At the censor's bidding, Anikieva's article was replaced with text by the more con-

1 L. Ivanova diary, 12 September 1934, call no. G94, IMRC. The diary—the surviving section—spans the period 1-26 September 1934 and reads as an inner dialogue with Vladislav Ravdonikas, Ivanova's third husband.
2 Ibid.
3 For an English translation of Vera Nikolaevna Anikieva's (1901-1941) essay on Filonov, see Nicoletta Misler and John E. Bowlt, *Pavel Filonov: A Hero and His Fate* (Austin, TX: Silvergirl, 1983), 53-68.

servative and academic Sergei Isakov.[4] The fact that Ivanova preserved both the Anikieva and the Isakov texts indicates not only her ongoing concern with Filonov, but also her bold disregard of the Secret Police inasmuch as the Anikieva essay was "politically incorrect," to say the least.

As to the absence of "the traces of infirmity, weakness, and technical retardation," then, this joyful outburst should be considered as implicit praise of the Filonov School. Ivanova's drawings and paintings of the time show a sniper's skill in graphic rendering, an impeccable sense of color, and a supreme control of paint. The thought of her impressions as narcissistic should be excluded because of the crisis of the moment, which entailed her sober opinion of her abilities. The ethical dimension of this opinion is explained fully by the following excerpts:

10 September 1934: Every sign of firmness and certainty of eye and hand is a joy for me, but not a joy from fame or dignity, but the serene joy of the master when he or she feels the blood rushing to the hands, and the power filling the pictures.... With the former joy you can oppress others and plunge in swaggering arrogance... But this is different, this is a feeling...which is deeply personal.[5]

However, just being ready to work hard is not enough. You have to set yourself a clear aim, i.e., the ultimate goal of any art, and dedicate yourself to the service of art, as Ivanova wished.

13 September 1934: Today I was in the Academy again. The stone has been prepared for me. I've chosen one of the drawings of Feodosii [in the Crimea] and I'll start on one of the autolithographs tomorrow. Everything goes as scheduled, on track, no changes. I'm beginning a new era. For all my tempestuous nature, I can now plan my actions...Uspensky and Pavlov promised to expose me to all kinds of studio graphics[6]...So there are still some good people in this world...When I left the Hermitage and joined AIMK, I decided that there were none left. But now everything is okay again.[7]

14 September 1934: Morning. Got up later than I should have because I went to bed late. I'd been looking through the clichés. In front of me stands a canvas. The sky troubles me. I want to draw. But, alas, I have to go off to the City Literature Office...Today I have to visit three publishing houses. At 5:00 p.m. they'll be waiting for me in the Academy...I won't go to the theater this evening, since I'm afraid that the new impressions will stand in the way of my 'painterly' concentration...Want to paint. Myriad thoughts, myriad desires, I am being drawn to the canvas. The smell of paints in the room. It excites me, it whets my desire to sit down and start working... Evening...Just came from the Academy...By 5:05 I was there. The stone was ready and, after stenciling in the drawing, I set to work. For three hours. Tomorrow I'll finish up...Day after tomorrow the first print will be done...I'm not going to the theater tomorrow either, even though I've been ordered a ticket...I'm afraid of forgetting the colors of the Crimea, of losing the immediate comprehension of what I saw, of becoming too theatralized...I feel flabby and passive.[8]

15 September 1934: Been to AIMK. They hold me in respect there... I'm so tired and troubled that I cannot work...Have to draw. Have to paint. Have to make up for lost time at breakneck speed. I'm 30 and I've done nothing. Have to make up. Pity that I didn't go to the theater.[9]

20 September 1934: I've just come back from the Academy and I brought with me (I'm so happy!) the first print of my lithograph. One print I gave Uspensky as a gift for his advice and help and I'll send you another tomorrow. It is not a full-colored print, but I'm so glad to have it...This evening I started and completed my next drawing—of Cherkes-Kermen...I now feel that my power of certainty and resolution are equal to that of 1921 when enrolled in the Academy...I never thought I'd ever experience this again, but there it is...Now I work without exaltation...it is a new stage, not joy and narcissism, but serious work. New, strong, and genuine. Henceforth, commence the throes of creativity.[10]

4   Sergei Konstantinovich Isakov (1875-1953), artist and art historian.
5   Ivanova diary, 10 September 1934.
6   Alexei Alexandrovich Uspensky (1892-1941) and Ivan Nikolaevich Pavlov (1872-1951) were leading engravers at the Academy of Arts.
7   Ivanova diary, 13 September 1934.
8   Ibid., 14 September 1934.
9   Ibid., 15 September 1934.
10 Ibid., 20 September 1934.

21 September 1934: I didn't work at the Academy today and I feel so depressed about it. I wanted to go there after the Party meeting, but I was afraid of finding everyone gone...I'll soon begin etching, which is going to be interesting. And they keep going on about linocuts.

The weather in Leningrad is wonderful...In the evening you can see an ocean of lights, cars are dashing by, trams are running. Crowds of noisy people...The sky is dark, but translucent in its blueness, the stars are sparkling and in the West the colors of the sky are slowly darkening. I love the city at this moment. Again, like many years ago, I walk out from the Academy and look at the River Neva bathed in lights.[11]

24 September 1934: I'm working...in a remarkable environment. Pavlov, Uspensky, Rudakov, Yudovin, Shillingovsky, Dobroklonsky, and others[12]...How amazing that until so recently I hated all artists... but now, after realizing who I am, I've started to understand and like this milieu and feel one of them...In general, this year is a new moment in my life. Both my social environment...and my private life—everything is new and different...Have grown up and become wise, wise, wise.[13]

9 September 1934: It's 8:00 p.m. In front of me on the table there is a pile of manuscripts and books that I brought home for editing. Many of them are very interesting...For today I gathered up the titles on Cézanne, on cinema, and on the actor Pudovkin (wonderful book, but with wrong methodology), on palace-museums, and, finally, one about resorts...After this, I'm faced with a thousand prints [to look at]...as well as a number of administrative projects for various publishing houses, clubs, and public education institutions...It's all piled up and it's all urgent...Today I reached an agreement with the Political Education Center. From early November on I'll be working there. They've set aside a studio for me—just for me personally.... We've decided to make the Center the same kind of art publishing house...as the State Visual Arts Publishing-House or LOSKh.[14]
So, here is Liudmila Ivanova, a Soviet Russian woman of the early 1930s! Her diverse roles as creative artist, political editor, censor, and supporter of the Communist Party of the Soviet Union formed

an explosive mixture. In the early 1930s, her strong vocabulary expressed a radical and progressive spirit, although today her revolutionary rhetoric (not unlike Filonov's slogans such as: "Make Way for Analytical Art!") sounds rather quaint. In the 1960s, my father, Vladislav Ravdonikas, confessed that he had seen the ideal modern woman in the thirty-year-old Ivanova.

This is an appropriate moment to recall that many of Filonov's students abandoned him and that none of them attained his level of mastery, perhaps because of the very dogmatism of the Analytical school. As Nietzsche once said: "A man of dogma is by necessity dependent, a man who is incapable of determining any goals for himself. He does not belong to himself, he can only be an instrument that somebody else must use."[15] However, we should not see Ivanova as the silent victim of doctrinal ambitions. Those who were close to her knew that she was ever ready to wrest with evil. Hers was a heroism that is manifest in the passages of her diary, often deeply private. The provocative reticence of this irrational and so Slavic lyricism only confirms what Joseph Brodsky once said: "language is not the instrument of cognition, but the instrument of appropriation."[16]

Henceforth, Ivanova found artistic truth in the archaeological expeditions of Ravdonikas, for whom she drew and painted the scenes that they encountered as he studied the primitive art of Northern Russia. While Ivanova traced impressions of petroglyphs, Ravdonikas, the brilliant comrade of the linguist and orientalist Nikolai Marr,[17] trod the path of the ancient prototype of the *Kalevala*, exploring and compiling data that are still of scientific value. These expeditions proved to be the happiest part of Ravdonikas's life as an archeologist while Ivanova found a new artistic beginning with her bold renderings of Lake Onezh and the White Sea.[18] Incidentally, the rock and cliff paintings there— the paleontology of the *Kalevala*—seem to be an exact and synthetic precedent to the "predicates"of Filonov's Analytical Art. One result of the Ravdonikas/Ivanova expeditions was that he was elected member of the Norwegian Academy of Sciences. A letter dated 5 August 1937 that Ravdonikas wrote during his expedition to Reindeer Island indi-

11 Ibid., 21 September 1934.

12 Konstantin Ivanovich Rudakov (1891-1949), Solomon Borisovich Yudovin (1894-1954), Pavel Alexandrovich Shillingovsky (1881-1942), and Viktor Viktorivich Dobroklonsky (1902-1960) were leading Academy artists in the 1930s.

13 Ivanova diary, 24 September 1934.

14 Ibid., 26 September 1934.

15 F. Nietzsche, "Ob antikhriste" [On the Anti-Christ] in *F. Nietzsche: Proiskhozhdenie tragedii. Ob antikhriste* (Moscow: 1900), 295.

16 I. Brodsky, "Na storone Kavafisa" in *Inostrannaia literatura* (Moscow: 1995), 12:209.

17 Nikolai Yakovlevich Marr (1864-1934), director of AIMK, achieved fame for his linguistic theories, which, however, were censured and condemned by Stalin.

cates the strength of their collaboration: "How I regret that you are not here.… So many interesting things. I'd like to record them all in form and color. Liuska, Liuska! You are the unique companion of my life. Not for bed, not for the home…but for work, for my vocation."[19]

The reformed Academy operated with a new system of so-called free, individual studios, open to all. There were no entrance examinations and any group of twenty or thirty students could invite this or that professor to be their supervisor and teach his particular system. Attendance at a higher educational institution exempted students from military obligations. Arkadii Rylov, then a young assistant at the reformed Academy, recalled:

More than fifteen individual studios opened, representing the most diverse orientations, from extreme right to extreme left. There was Tatlin's studio with its denotation "Construction, Space and Material" and Matiushin's with his theory of "expanded vision." In Tatlin's studio there were anvils, a joiner's bench, and metalwork equipment instead of easels, palettes, and brushes and students constructed things out of different materials such as wood, metal, and mica. The few students in Matiushin's studio had to paint according to the method of "expanded vision" not only what was before them, but also what was behind, to the side, above, and below. Natan Altman taught surface-texture painting without chiaroscuro, adding sand or bran to the paint or even burning the surface. Ivan Puni favored still-lifes with curved pitchers, plates, and pots, gluing pieces of newspaper, rope, and wooden sticks to the canvas…K. S. Petrov-Vodkin's studio was very popular with his specific "three color-system" and spherical perspective…There was also the studio without a teacher and professor. "What is anatomy for and what is perspective for?" Tatlin would ask.[20]

Perhaps Nikolai Punin tried to answer this question in his lectures on the "the history of artistic culture."

Of more consequence were Ivanova's encounters with Filonov in 1924 or 1925. According to her, time spent in his studio lost all connection with real time. Her apartment on the opposite side of the Neva (now building number 22 on the English Quay) did not escape Filonovization and the space became a club for the Filonovians.[21]

Filonov's personality as a great artist also acquired an accretion of the legendary. From childhood I heard stories from my mother about Filonov, the one who despised any commercial function, who made his own boots to keep within his ascetic economy. In my student years, my mother contended that the drawings of Evgenii Kibrik and Valentin Kurdov were successful precisely because of their Filonovian experience. Filonov used to evoke the image of birds who could not fly if their strength was concentrated in the left or the right wing. Citing Filonov, she explained how drawings should be made from nature and her own student drawings were ample proof that she had succeeded in appropriating that tradition—an analytical force manifest in the designs that she made on commission for cigarette packages.

It is hard to conclude which of the Analytical graphic pieces is the most accomplished. According to Ivanova's own words, not all of them were done during her student years and she still manifested a rugged independence in her contribution to the collective for the *Kalevala* publication in 1933. Not counting a large canvas from the Cherkes-Kermen series,[22] the wonderful oil portrait of 1931, symbol of a daughter's grief at the passing of her mother, is surely the last of the major Analytical works by Ivanova.

18 See V. Ravdonikas, *Naskalnye izobrazheniia Onezhskogo ozera i Belogo moria* [Cliff Drawings of Lake Onezh and the White Sea] (Moscow, Leningrad: Academy of Arts of USSR, Vol. 1, 1936; Vol. 2, 1938). Ivanova designed and illustrated both volumes and provided two landscapes for the frontispieces. According to Ivanova's diary of 25 October 1942 (author's archive), "The First Volume ["Petroglyphic Images"] was [exhibited] at the Paris Exposition of 1937 [and] awarded a medal. These books were reprinted in France with complete reproduction of the artistic designs and illustrations."

19 In 1991 Ravdonikas's letters were donated to Leningrad University Museum.

20 A. Rylov, *Vospominaniia* (Moscow, Leningrad: Ogiz-Izogiz, 1940), 161-163. Rylov is referring to the artists Natan Isaevich Altman (1889-1970), Mikhail Vasilievich Matiushin (1861-1934), Kuzma Sergeevich Petrov-Vodkin (1878-1939), and Vladimir Evgrafovich Tatlin (1885-1953).

21 Ivanova painted several views from this apartment in 1924-1925. Of the original members of the Filonov School, Evgenii Adolfovich Kibrik (1906-1978) and Valentin Ivanovich Kurdov (1905-1989) seem to have been closest to her.

22 This Cherkes-Kermen landscape has not survived, although its disappearance is a mystery inasmuch as Ivanova guarded her Academy and Analytical works jealously and never showed them to anyone, not even to me.

Why Her? Why Here?

PETER FRANK

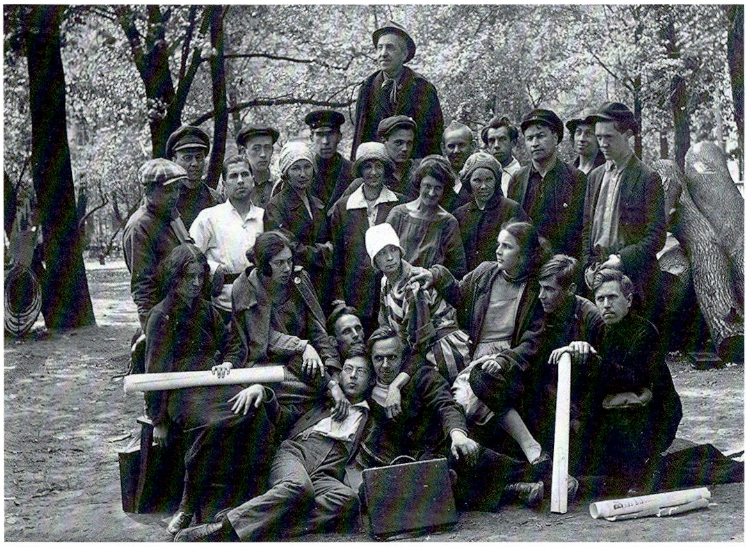

Fig. 3 Matiushin's Second Year Class (G7) May 20, 1925
Ivanova seated front row, far left.

In recent decades, the astounding achievement of the Russian avant-garde has been subject to several waves of reexamination, the newest one taking advantage of the wider access that historians now have to museums, archives, and private estates in Russia and the other nations of the Council of Independent States (the former Soviet republics). Among other results of this latest reassessment, is the emergence of an enhanced appreciation for the vanguard activity in centers other than Moscow—activity not exported from that revolutionary hub as part of the new government's attempt to radicalize the entire fabric of Russian society, but *sui generis*, native to its locale, and often pre-Revolutionary in origin. In this way, we are becoming more aware of a Dada cell in Odessa; Marc Chagall can be understood as part of an anti-academic circle in Vitebsk; pockets of experiment in Kiev, Baku, Vilnius, Tbilisi, and other outposts of the old Empire emerge as more than mere satellites of Moscovian modernism; Leningrad, now returned to its original title of St. Petersburg, has regained its stature as "the other" center of Soviet experimental modernism.

Recognized as the second hub of Russian vanguard art before the Revolution, Petrograd—the capital of tsarist Russia—did not fade into desuetude as the weeds overcame its Czarist monuments. Many of Petrograd's artistic revolutionaries remained loyal to their hometown and its traditions—even managing the coherent transition of its Academy of Arts into the Soviet era, saving the venerable institution from dissolution at the hands of iconoclastic bureaucrats by reforming its pedagogical structure. The Academy (where Mikhail Matiushin, Kuzma Petrov-Vodkin *inter alia* were teaching after 1918) was the obvious forum where students could be exposed to avant-garde ideas—ideas which were debated and expanded at the think-tank known as Ginkhuk.

Arising from the Museum of Artistic Culture founded in 1918, Ginkhuk operated as a research center from 1923 until 1926, attracting some of the leading lights of the artistic revolution. Under the directorship of Kazimir Malevich (also head of the Department of Form and Theory), Ginkhuk encouraged theoretical and practical investigation in a variety of æsthetic, stylistic, and material areas via the Department of Experimentation (headed by Pavel Mansurov), the

Department of Organic Culture (headed by Matiushin), and the Department of General Ideology (headed by Pavel Filonov and, later, the critic Nikolai Punin). Within and without the Academy and Ginkhuk, Petrograd avant-gardists such as Filonov and Matiushin propagated their theories and methods (which were, to say the least, very personal, cryptic, and complex) in and through their own studios. Filonov in particular—whose eccentricities and contentious attitudes about art and life are as bewildering as they are appealing—always worked best in the immediate environment of his own home.

Indeed, after earning her degree at the Academy in 1926, Liudmila Ivanova established close contact with Filonov and her most unusual works from this time evince the master's unmistakable approach. True, the almost pathological obsessiveness and grotesque morbidity of Filonov's own painting and drawing are absent from Ivanova's work; but, in her adoption of what Filonov called the Art of Universal Flowering, Ivanova demonstrated that his unique concepts were not entirely inimitable to and might even inform more mainstream visual praxes in the applied as well as fine arts. Actually, to judge from exhibition designs that she devised as curator at the Russian Museum and other institutions in the late 1920s and early 1930s, Ivanova seems to have been influenced more by Matiushin's diagrammatic method of elucidation; she did, nonetheless, contribute to the Russian edition of the Finnish epos *Kalevala* that the Filonov school illustrated in 1933.

Filonov was not the only major influence on Ivanova: her tenure under Matiushin prompted an interest in that artist-musician's powerful theories about form and color—Ivanova even applied these theories to the traditional landscape format, rather as Matiushin himself had done so before the Revolution. Certainly, her works were more conservative than the abstracted "landscapes" realized by Matiushin himself and his closest acolytes, such as the Ender family.[1] Ivanova's efforts under Petrov-Vodkin, in turn, recapitulated his circumspect Cubism, a "re-academicization" of Picasso and Braque's original system.[2]

Once Ivanova retreated into the intimate landscape compositions of the 1930s, what she learned from Matiushin and Petrov-Vodkin stood her in greater stead than what she learned from Filonov. Still, Ivanova produced her most distinctive work under Filonov's guidance; and if her Matiushin-like pastels resemble the misty, halted Symbolist landscapes manufactured across *fin de siècle* Europe and if her homage to Petrov-Vodkin recapitulates his moderate Cubism, her Filonovian sketches—dense, shivering, unstable, so crammed with images that they turn recessional space into directionless, multiplanar interiors of crystals—seem unprecedented—except for Filonov's own work, which they reflect and interpret.

An increasing number of scholars have been arguing the cases of Filonov and Matiushin—rabid, theorists and practitioners whose relative obscurity now seems a result of geography, language, and, in all likelihood, the peculiarity (at least to Western minds) of their curious theories. It is the fantastic quality of these theories, together with their thoroughness and actual basis in empirical reason, that makes them of interest to our Post-Modernist discourse; arguably, it is their conflation of rational measure with an almost hallucinatory extrapolation that make them so "Russian." Both as souvenirs of these theories and as general essays in Modernist abstraction—notably as manifestations of personal inspiration rather than ideological programs—Filonov's and Matiushin's artwork merit consideration alongside Vasilii Kandinsky's, Paul Klee's, Frantisek Kupka's, and Arthur Dove's. Petrov-Vodkin's more modest contribution, too, is beginning to receive attention, not least as a curious bridge between avant-garde and academic practices, one which sustained a number of Leningrad artists who wished to avoid rather than serve the artistic behests of the state during the long Stalinist night.

If we can agree that Ivanova's *œuvre* merits kinder treatment than dispersion through small auction houses, museum depositories, antique stores, and thrift shops, we have to ask why. Why are academic organizations such as the Institute of Modern Russian

1 Boris Vladimirovich Ender (1893-1960), Ksenia Vladimirovna (1895-1965), and Mariia Vladimirovna (1897-1942) were eager students of Matiushin, elaborating his color and space theories and applying them to their own interpretations of non-objective painting.

2 For information on Matiushin and the Enders, see Alla Povelikhina, ed., *Matjuschin und die Leningrader Avantgarde*, ex. cat. (Karlsruhe: Zentrum für Kunst und Medientechnologie, 1991); and *Organica*, ex. cat. (Cologne: Galerie Gmurzynska, 1999). For further information on Ivanova and Matiushin and Petrov-Vodkin, see Alina Orlov, "The Late Landscaped: Remembering Mikhail Matiushin" and David Borgmeyer, "'A Certainty of Eye and Hand:' Ivanova and Kuzma Petrov-Vodkin" in this catalog.

Culture and the Fisher Gallery at the University of Southern California, Los Angeles, undertaking the preservation and documentation of this body of work, and why are they devoting many resources to creating a scholarly exhibition of it. Why her? Why here?

The reasons for working with and exhibiting the Ivanova estate go well beyond the merits of the work itself. Is she being presented here as a stalking horse for the rehabilitation of her teachers? No; they have been better served by displays of their own work in the context of the Russian avant-garde in general. Is this presentation simply a matter of promoting an unfamiliar name to a narrow academic audience? Hardly; with their extensive contacts and history of trusted cooperation with artists and museum people in Russia, the IMRC and the Fisher Gallery are quite capable of assembling a stellar array of primary works by the Russian avant-garde. Rather, acceptance of the Ivanova gift in 1989 was entirely in keeping with the purview of the IMRC—which is to examine the function of modern Russian/Soviet art precisely in its social and societal contexts.

Ivanova's modest talent and inquiring mind are, in fact, perfect grist for our mill. She typifies the would-be experimentalist among the first generation of artists educated in, and nurtured by, the Soviet Union. Her life and work are entirely framed by Soviet reality, the Communist Party, and the rigors of Stalin's regime. In effect, the Ivanova bequest provides us with the opportunity to reconstruct a life and career characteristic of many other lives and careers during the time and place to which her artwork bears ready testimony.

In the context of Post-Modernist historicism, the investigation and revelation of Ivanova's life and art tells us much about the art and society in which she participated. Indeed, it tells us more about the interaction of that art and society than might the work and life of any of her teachers. Of course, Matiushin, Petrov-Vodkin, and Filonov were also products and reflections of their era; but examination of this era through their art may cause a distortion that Ivanova's clearer lens does not. Although we cannot adequately understand that era without studying Ivanova's teachers, we cannot understand that era by studying them alone. Matiushin, Filonov, and, to a lesser extent, Petrov-Vodkin, affected rather than refracted their time and place.

Post-modernist historiography recognizes that concentration on the "great men" of history has a Heisenbergian effect on the comprehension of history, amplifying and suppressing information according to its proximity to these celebrities. An artist or artistic totality such as Ivanova, however, comes much closer to moving through history, recording its marks and imprints without in turn affecting it in a way that would obscure the nature of its evolution.

The Institute preserves Ivanova's artworks and writings as archival documents; thus, for the purposes of "Myriad Thoughts, Myriad Desires," works that required restoration have been restored according to the most sensitive and exacting techniques as objects of museum quality should be. True, many of the drawings, at least, would be valued by collectors for their cultural curiosity, historical interest, and æsthetic quality. Perhaps some of the works do belong on view outside the context of the bequest. If a museum of modern Russian art, for instance, were to be modeled on the radical curatorial example of the Musée d'Orsay in Paris, certain of Ivanova's student works could hang quite logically next to the Filonovs and Matiushins and a later landscape or two could be included in the gentle non-propagandistic figuration that would surround the requisite bombastic murals of workers and farmers, Mongols and Tatars gathered round a gesticulating Lenin or a far-gazing Stalin.

So do these considerations justify the exhibition of selected works from the bequest and the mounting of an Ivanova retrospective? Does not a show of this kind infer an upward reevaluation—not just out of total obscurity, but into a merited exposure in the official exhibition space of a leading university in one of the world's major art centers? Here is a survey of an artist who may be more significant for what she assimilated than for what she produced, but our very focus on Ivanova underscores the particular kind of value that her work holds. On its own, that work deserves exposure, however mild its rewards. Macrocosmically, however, this very mildness makes Ivanova's art of more than passing interest. It may not be "great art," but it is certainly "good" and it is eminently symptomatic of a particular time, of a particular place, of a particular group of people operating within, affected by, and affecting a particular society.

Ivanova may or may not have manifested the signal characteristics of "genius," but she did something which, we now recognize, is valuable in its own right: she generated a body of work responsive to, and reflective of, the artistic discourse of her day, and she kept that body of work together. Ivanova is a one-woman cross-section of Leningrad Modernism (and anti-Modernism) and she provides us a uniquely coherent comprehension of her time.

Firing the Canon:
Ivanova and the Myth of the
Russian Avant-Garde

RAIMOND LIVASGANI

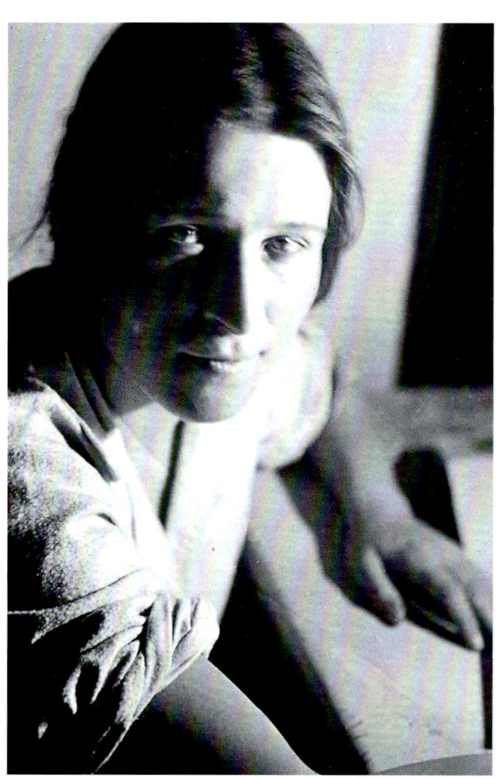

Fig. 4 Liudmila Ivanova (G15) c. 1920s

Art exhibitions and their mandates depend as much on the works exhibited as their venues. As mediators between the objects on display and the audience, museums are invested with an authority of interpretation arising from the professional training of their curators and staff. In creating narratives around objects, museums subtly or openly reveal their ideological positions. The exhibitions hosted by museums are expected not only to contribute to institutionalized stories but also to the particular story of the institution. "Myriad Thoughts, Myriad Desires" fulfills both expectations, offering an alternative approach to the history of Russian Modernism and its exhibition, while also declaring the purpose and mission of the Fisher Gallery itself. Furthermore, "Myriad Thoughts, Myriad Desires" provides an opportunity to grapple with pressing art historical and museological issues that echo throughout current Post-Modernist discourse by exposing the works of Liudmila Ivanova, an unfamiliar figure in Russian Modernism.[1]

What did inspire our research team to mobilize their resources for an exhibition of an unknown Russian female artist at the USC Fisher Gallery?[2] What kind of debates ensue when a museum contests the established canons of art history in its search for a fresh perspective on an accepted historical narrative? How is this exhibition informative in ways that differ from other exhibitions pertaining to Russian Modernism, such as "The Avant-Garde in Russia 1910-1930. New Perspectives" (Los Angeles County Museum of Art and the Hirshchorn Museum and Sculpture Garden, 1980-1981) or the "Great Utopia" (Solomon R. Guggenheim Museum and other venues in 1992-1993)? "Myriad Thoughts, Myriad Desires" differs from these and other exhibitions of Russian Modernism by revisiting traditional exhibiting practices and their impact on the scholarly discourse and by exploring the relevance—or irrelevance—of, e.g., issues of gender and marginality as negotiated within and by the museum.

Unlike the canonical history of Western art, which until recently neglected the impact of female artists, the discourse on Russian culture of the Silver Age and the avant-garde (ca. 1895-1925) affirms that women artists made crucial contributions to artistic

1   For useful discussions of current exhibition and museological practices in the United States, see Bruce Altshuler, *The Avant-Garde in Exhibition: New Art in the 20th Century* (Berkeley: University of California Press, 1994); Reesa Greenberg, Bruce W. Ferguson, and Sandy Nairne, eds., *Thinking About Exhibitions* (New York: Routledge, 1996); and Didier Maleuvre, *Museum Memories. History, Technology,* Art (Palo Alto, CA: Stanford University Press, 1999).
2   "Myriad Thoughts, Myriad Desires" is the first museum retrospective of Liudmila Ivanova's works. In 1990, Karen Meyers curated a selected exhibition at the IMRC entitled "The Knowing Eye" (catalog) and three of Ivanova's works were included in the 1990 exhibition "Pavel Filonov und seine Schule" at the Kunsthalle, Dusseldorf.

procedures—exhibitions, institutions, publications—and were certainly not excluded because of gender.[3] Even as the avant-garde gave way to a more conservative style, culminating in the triumph of Socialist Realism under Stalin, the influence of women seems not to have waned. After all, the sculptors Sarra Lebedeva and Vera Mukhina, both of whom were active before and after 1917, had greatly affected the creation of the new and powerful iconography of the proletarian hero. Active in the modernist circles of St. Petersburg, Lebedeva moved alongside with such luminaries as the poets Alexander Blok and Vladimir Maiakovsky and the artists Kazimir Malevich and Vladimir Tatlin and responded enthusiastically to Lenin's Plan of Monumental Propaganda in 1918. Similarly, Mukhina received the 1937 commission for the design of the enormous stainless steel statue of a Worker and Collective Farm Woman for the Soviet Pavilion at the Paris Exposition; while not immune to political censure, Mukhina continued to create and exhibit during the Stalinist era. These examples would seem to contradict or, at least, qualify, the declaration by the late Miuda Yablonskaya, a leading Moscow art historian, that the Soviet establishment was suppressing female participation in cultural life by the mid-1930s.[4] In other words, Ivanova's apparent marginality may stem not from her gender, but from a more complex set of circumstances—such as her association with St. Petersburg, Russia's "second" city, and with artists (Pavel Filonov, Mikhail Matiushin, Kuzma Petrov-Vodkin) whose names are still less familiar in Western scholarship than those of Malevich, Tatlin, and Rodchenko.

Ivanova's marginal status may also have been affected by the fact that she stood at a momentous juncture in the development of Russian art: between the cultural effervescence of the pre-Revolutionary avant-garde and the unforgiving regime of Stalin's dictatorship, between æsthetic tolerance and plurality and the monolithic establishment of Socialist Realism. But Ivanova can be accommodated in neither one nor the other category, a duality symbolized by her abrupt and contradictory stylistic changes after 1934. Prior to that year, her works echo the stylistic features of her teachers, especially Filonov's Analytical Art (his system of Universal Flowering) and Matiushin's space-color perception. By the mid-1930s, however, all traces of Filonov have vanished from both the formal resolution of her work and its subject-matter.[5] True, the later works, whether landscapes or figures, betray the influence of Petrov-Vodkin and Matiushin, but it is slight and elusive.[6]

In considering Ivanova in relation to the avant-garde (or Socialist Realists), it is important to remember that "avant-garde" and "Socialist Realism" are packaging labels that reduce art to the marketing status of intellectual goods; such packaging creates overly narrow categories that exclude or distort artists like Ivanova. Many Russian artists of the early twentieth century did not call themselves avant-garde:[7] there may have been common ground, but there was no one unified body called "the avant-garde" (suffice it to remember the constant antagonism between Malevich and Tatlin). The term avant-garde or, rather, its fashionable use, is a later concoction, coined to facilitate and empower the treatment of what appears to be a contemporary body of artists with various objectives united only by their dissent from the preceding academic system.[8] In exhibitions devoted to the avant-garde, the artist tends to be mythologized as superman, petrifiying the concept of avant-garde

3   Natalia Goncharova, for example, had comprehensive one-woman exhibitions in Moscow and St. Petersburg in 1913 and 1914; Liubov Popova, Olga Rozanova, and Nadezhda Udaltsova contributed to major avant-garde exhibitions in the 1910s; and women played a major role at the conclusive—pre-Constructivism—exhibition, "5 x 5 = 25" in Moscow in 1910. For more information on the prominent role of women in modern Russian art, see John E. Bowlt and Matthew Drutt, eds., *Amazonen der Avant-Garde. Amazons of the Avant-Garde.* ex. cat. (Berlin: Deutsche Guggenheim, 1999).

4   Myuda Yablonskaya, *Women Artists of Russia's New Age 1900-1935* (London: Thames and Hudson, 1990), 12.

5   See Felix Ravdonikas, "My Mother, Liudmila Ivanova," in this catalog. In Ivanova's diary entry, 12 September 1934, she refers to "those terrible… Filonovian mugs."

6   For further information on Ivanova and Filonov, Matiushin, and Petrov-Vodkin see Nicoletta Misler, "Restless Skies," Alina Orlov, "The Late Landscapes: Remembering Mikhail Matiushin," and David Borgmeyer, "'A Certainty of Eye and Hand:' Ivanova and Kuzma Petrov-Vodkin" in this catalog.

7   Some members of the "Russian" avant-garde were not ethnically "Russian," hailing from Armenia, Georgia, Latvia, Lithuania, Poland, the Ukrain, etc.

8   The first use of the term "avant-garde" in reference to the experimental art movements in Moscow and St. Petersburg seems to have occurred in Alexandre Benois's exhibition review of "Union of Russian Artists" in February 1910 which included works by Pavel Kuznetsov, Mikhail Larionov, and Georgii Yakulov. See M. Etkind, *A.N. Benois i russkaia khudozhestvennaia kultura* (Leningrad: Khudozhnik RSFSR, 1989), 187.

through an emphasis on the position of pioneering artists such as
Natalia Goncharova, Mikhail Larionov, Malevich, and Tatlin. This
organization of knowledge has prompted scholars to demarcate the
parameters within which art-historical investigations are pursued.
However, the often unheeded danger is that in creating a semblance of continuous historical narrative from the study of fragments and its packaging, we have developed and concentrated
upon a single discourse around seminal and salient figures. These
celebrities may deserve their status, but not at the expense of liminal figures and places such as Ivanova in St. Petersburg. Thus,
while exposing Ivanova's *œuvre*, we refrain from accommodating
her within any one school, a reluctance dictated in part by the
resistance of her work to easy stylistic categorization.

"Myriad Thoughts, Myriad Desires" offers a new entrée into the
plight of the marginalized artist and into the concept of the "other"
and the "peripheral." This exhibition is as much about issues related to the rediscovery of obscure artists in general as it is about
Ivanova herself. While not downplaying the significance of her association with the avant-gardists of St. Petersburg /Leningrad such as
Filonov and Matiushin, this study helps to explain that, ultimately,
the invisibility of an artist may have nothing to do with his or her
creative talent and artistic originality. Ivanova seems never to have
contributed to public exhibitions. Why? Did she not see herself as a
professional artist? Or did she consider her work to be so anti-insti-
tutional that, if shown publicly, the work would be subject to criticism, even condemnation and herself to physical danger?[9] Yet, in
the early 1930s she worked as a political editor and research assistant at AIMK—biographical facts that point to her accomodation
with the political regime. Can we account for such apparent contradictions? Although in her mature period she hardly promoted or
elaborated their styles, she was nonetheless informed by the artistic systems of Filonov, Matiushin, and Petrov-Vodkin. On the other
hand, with her mild landscapes and occasional spontaneous portraits, she was not a Socialist Realist and seems not to have championed the state's appeal for an art that was both a tendentious
and a didactic instrument.

"Myriad Thoughts, Myriad Desires" treats Ivanova simply as an
artist active in the last years of the avant-garde—but this treatment
distinguishes the exhibition from most of those devoted to Russian
modernism. Ivnaova was neither a Moscovite nore a celebrated
artist; these are the facts that allow the study of Ivanova to broaden
our understanding of the breadth of "modernist" production in
Russia as well as our estimation of artists active outside of Moscow,
for example in St. Petersburg or Saratov.[10]

Three exhibition practices seem to dominate the exposure and advocacy of the Russian avant-garde: reliance upon private collections
(e.g., "Art of the Avant-Garde in Russia: Selections from the George
Costa's Collection" organized by the Solomon R. Guggenheim in
1981); identification with a specific time span ("Art in Revolution.
Soviet Art and Design since 1917" organized at the Hayward Gallery,
London, in 1971); and general, often piece-meal compilations (such
as "Russian Art of the Revolution" at the Brooklyn Museum in 1971).
Regardless of the format, all three practices tend to focus on the
activities of major figures; even "Amazons of the Avant-Garde," which
opened at the Deutsche Guggenheim in Berlin in July 1999, differs
only in its concern for the established female contributors to the
avant-garde, namely, Alexandra Exter, Natalia Goncharova, Liubov
Popova, Olga Rozanova, Varvara Stepanova, and Nadezhda Udaltsova.
One recent exhibition does seem to depart from the generic presentation of the Russian avant-garde; according to Christina Lodder, "New
Art for a New Era: Malevich's Vision of the Russian Avant-Garde"
(which opened at the Barbican Art Gallery, London in June 1999)
included an impressive number of woman artists whose creative contribution equaled and often surpassed that of the their male colleagues. Even this exhibition, however, was packaged as Malevich's
vision: "Highlighting him," Lodder writes, "makes sense in marketing
terms: but in terms of history it is misleading."[11]

An exhibition such as "Myriad Thoughts, Myriad Desires" may help
rectify this historical imbalance, all the more so as it takes place in
a museum, not a commercial gallery. Museums have greater cultural and institutional authority to permit entrance into the (art)-his-

---

9 In the sense that she declined to exhibit her work in public institutions, Ivanova may be considered "avant-garde."
   Consciously or not, she may have been heeding Marinetti's earlier appeal to destroy museums before the new art
   could be created.

10 For information on Russian avant-garde works, including paintings by lesser known artists such as Alexei Rybnikov
   and Mikhail Veksler (a student of Kazimir Malevich), in regional museums, see Andrei Sarabianov and Nina
   Gurianova, *Neizvestnyi russkii avangard* (Moscow: Sovetskii khudozhnik, 1992).

11 Christina Lodder, "New Art for a New Era: Malevich's Vision of the Russian Avant-Garde," Burlington Magazine CXLI,
   1156 (July 1999): 428.

torical discourse than commercially-motivated galleries. Museums are one site of entry into discourse of art history; but, as Mieke Bal has stressed, the "museum is a discourse, and exhibition an utterance within that discourse."[12] Other exhibitions have offered surveys and overviews of the avant-garde; our intention, however, is to present a critical body of work in an innovative setting that encourages the viewer's engagement and helps fashion an unconventional counter-narrative.

This exhibition was made possible only due to the accessibility of the Ivanova collection at the IMRC, but two principal motivations drove it: the desire to mount the first comprehensive public display of Ivanova's work and the desire to expose and underline the limitations of the art historical canons of classification. By drawing attention to a liminal or "secondary" artist, this exhibition may intervene in the process of the commodification of Russian Modernism, especially as the history of Russian art is a relatively new discipline. Furthermore, the collaboration between the Museum Studies Program, the IMRC, and the Department of Slavic Languages and Literatures at the University of Southern California, Los Angeles, provides a model of a more porous and synthetic approach to the study of art history than the rigid borders of individual disciplines; the exhibition itself is ample testimony that an interdisciplinary approach is essential for a fair and accurate interpretation of art history.

"Myriad Thoughts, Myriad Desires" maintains the Fisher Gallery's strong position at the forefront of museological and art historical discourse. It is a dedication manifest in the Gallery's policies of acquisition and collection (for instance, the ongoing purchasing of works by Chicano artists) as well as in the organization of exhibitions such as the "Keepers of the Flame: Unofficial Artists of Leningrad" (1990-1991)[13]—an exhibition which, incidentally, resembles the Ivanova show in two important ways: it presented artists who were nonconformists and outside the mainstream, but also who, like Ivanova, were from Russia's "second city," St. Petersburg/Leningrad.

12 Mieke Bal, "The Discourse of the Museum," in *Thinking About Exhibitions*, eds. Reesa Greenberg, Bruce W. Ferguson, and Sandy Nairne (New York: Routledge, 1996), 214.
13 "Keepers of the Flame. Unofficial artists of Leningrad," (catalog) 14 November 1990 through 19 January 1991. Exhibition traveled to Emmerson Gallery, Hamilton College in Clinton, NY, and to the Berman Museum of Art, Ursinus College, Collegeville, PA.

The Politics of Style

RANDI HOKETT

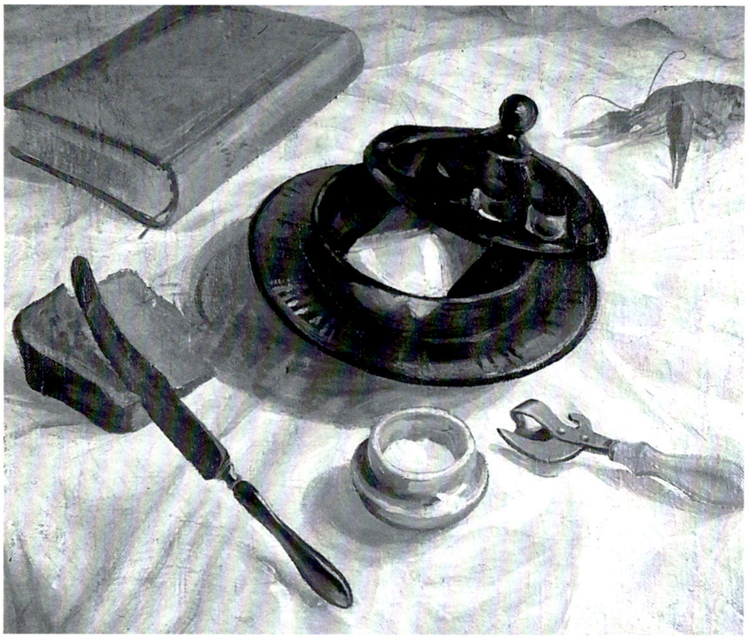

Fig. 5 Still Life with Bread and Butter (F47) mid-1920s

How do we begin to understand an artist whose *œuvre* has been largely disregarded, if not ignored? An artist whose work changes drastically in what seems to be only a matter of years? More importantly, what does such an artist's work offer to the larger discourse of art history?

The artistic achievement of Liudmila Ivanova, while perhaps not equal to that of such pioneers of the Russian avant-garde as Pavel Filonov, Natalia Goncharova, or Kazimir Malevich, provides valuable insight both into the notion of the "peripheral" artist and into the complex period in which she worked. Indeed, to a considerable extent, Ivanova's art functions to the modern viewer as a pedagogical tool, which allows us to understand some of the fundamental changes that occurred in early twentieth century Russia and also how these changes informed and affected a specific artist's work. Far from reflecting the conventional notion of Russian propagandistic imagery, Ivanova's work declares her belief in the proletariat and the new society by a subtler means.

Ivanova's art echoes a sincere, personal belief in the Socialist structure and stands as a testament to the condition of Russian culture in the early decades of the twentieth century. Although formally her work moves from Analytical Art (her interpretations of Filonov's system) to a version of Socialist Realism, it always suggests a genuine love of the artistic process—as well as a ready support of the Party or, at least, of the Soviet regime. This support is a very important aspect of Ivanova's career, her *œuvre*, and this exhibition. After all, at the time of the Bolshevik Revolution Ivanova was only thirteen and must have been deeply affected by that experience. The express intent of the revolution was to tear down an imperialist structure and to replace it with a proletarian dictatorship. Ultimately, the Bolsheviks hoped to eliminate the class system by giving priority to the needs of the collective, rather than the individual; one of the principal instruments of this social transformation was culture.

Approaches to the issue of a proletarian art were numerous. As early as 1918, Alexander Andreev, a member of the Petrograd Proletkult and a professor at the Academy of Arts, identified the

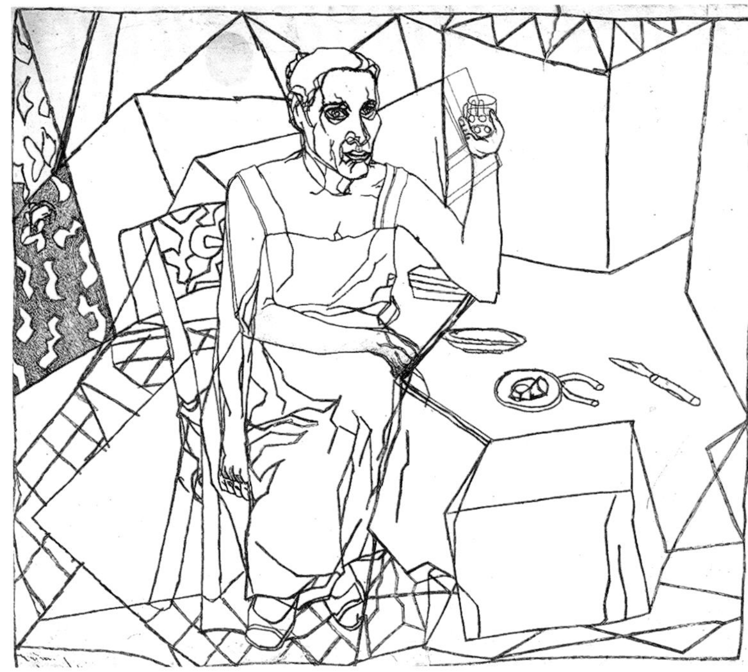

role of art in the revolution: "Through art, we must inculcate elements of clear understanding of the world into the consciousness of the masses, an awareness that the time of Socialism is coming about through the proletarian commune."[1] In the years following the revolution, different artistic factions claimed to represent the art of the people and Ivanova experimented with their styles, including those of Filonov, Mikhail Matiushin, and Kuzma Petrov-Vodkin. Filonov, in particular, believed that anyone could learn the methods of Analytical Art and that this, therefore, was the true art of the proletariat; Ivanova supported that notion, at least when she was close to Filonov in the late 1920s.

In 1918, the Academy of Art was transformed into the Svomas—a system of free studios open to everyone. Teachers such as Matiushin represented the avant-garde and, although their classes were not especially popular, they influenced Ivanova's work. Matiushin taught his students a system of "expanded-vision" which purportedly allowed the artist to see above, below, behind, and to the left and right of the normal line of vision. Tatlin's studio used wood, metal, and other materials to create purely visual compositions. Petrov-Vodkin was already working with a system that emphasized pure colors—blue, red, and yellow. On the other hand, Dmitrii Kardovskii, Arkadii Rylov, and Vasilii Savinskii, among others championed Realism in their studios. Svomas was disbanded in 1921, the year of Ivanova's enrollment, and replaced by Vkhutemas, whose hallmark was a system in which a collective of two or three professors taught classes. In 1925, Petrov-Vodkin was invited to institute his three-color system at the Academy; Ivanova received part of her official art education in accordance with this system, which she utilized throughout her life (for instance, in her 1930s *Still Life with Bread and Butter*, fig. 5, F47).

After attending the Academy, Ivanova took lessons from Filonov, who seems to have exerted the strongest influence upon her artistic evolution. From him, Ivanova learned Analytical Art, a method which incorporated the sciences and states of matter such as crystallography, biology, and decomposition. *Woman at Table Holding Glass* (fig. 6, C1) is an early example of Ivanova's use of the Analytical method. Here she employs strong lines to produce the

appearance of decomposition; the woman's body seems to cave in on itself while the sunken depth around her eyes creates a skeletal impression.

Ivanova graduated from the Academy in 1926 to take up a curatorial appointment in painting and sculpture at the State Russian Museum, where she later edited posters for the Leningrad division of the Visual Arts Publishing House. In the years 1931-1933, she attended graduate school at the Hermitage in the Department of European Art, where she also worked as an installer. In 1933-1934, Ivanova functioned as a scholarly worker at the Marr State Academy of Material Culture (AIMK). Perhaps because of these obligations, Ivanova produced few paintings during the period 1926-1934. In her diary entry for 12 September 1934, she describes weeping at the joy of painting in oil after a hiatus of ten years.

With some exceptions, the chronology of the works in the IMRC archive coincides with this time-line. Judging from Ivanova's predominant style in the 1930s, she seems to have experienced an ideological shift, rejecting Analytical Art, and turning her attention instead to the Russian landscape. Several factors would seem to have contributed to this development. From the late 1920s onward,

1   Alexander Andreev, "On the Question of Fine Arts" (1918) in *Bolshevik Visions: The First Phase of the Cultural Revolution in Soviet Russia*, 2nd ed. (Part 2, Creating Soviet Cultural Forms: Art, Architecture, Film and the New Tasks of Education), ed. W. Rosenberg (Ann Arbor: University of Michigan Press, 1990). Alexander Alexandrovich Andreev (1887-1941) was a painter and designer with a particular interest in proletarian art education and appreciation.

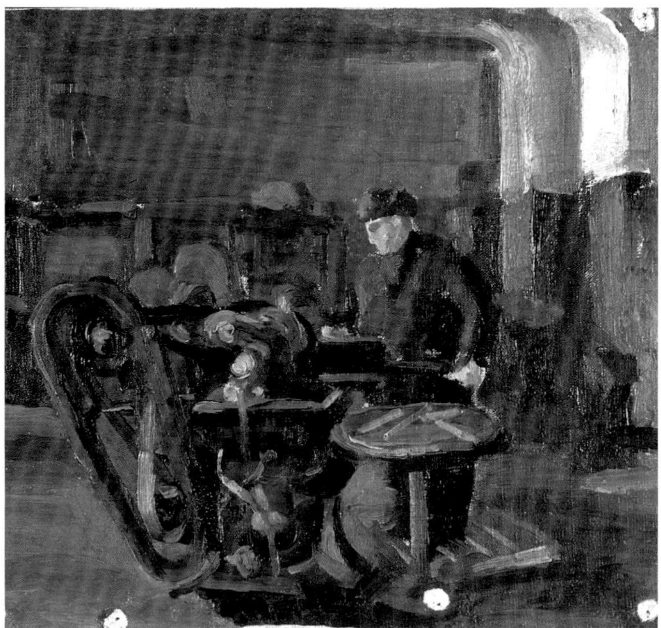

Fig. 7 Worker in Factoryshop (F35) late1930s

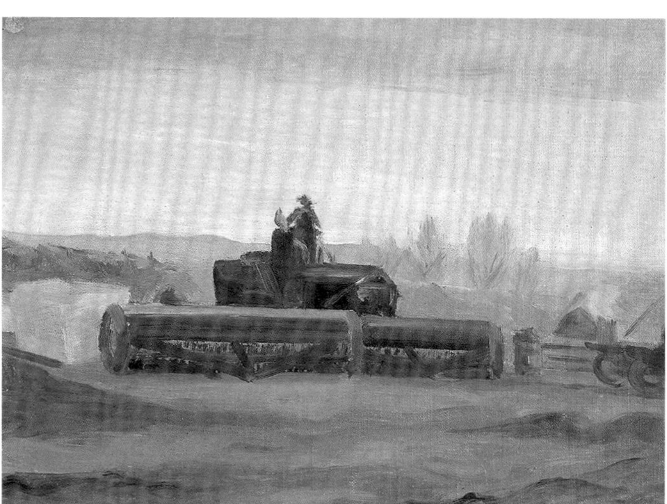

Fig. 8 Farm Scene with Tractor (F18) mid-1930s

Stalin relentlessly sought to eradicate opposition: "persons propagating opposition views were to be regarded as dangerous accomplices of the external and internal enemies of the Soviet Union…. Everyone who arouses the slightest suspicion should be removed."[2] However much the avant-gardists had proclaimed their art to be that of the proletariat, they were now considered to be politically unreliable, if not seditious. The resulting repression even touched the loyal Ivanova with the arrest in 1937 of her second husband, the artist Nikolai Kuranov.

Working at the State Russian Museum, Ivanova also witnessed the intrigues and duplicity that surrounded the "non-exhibition" of Filonov's works.[3] Set to open in 1929, the exhibition was never officially unveiled because Filonov's work had come to be regarded as subversive and alien to the proletariat. Much to Filonov's displeasure, Vera Anikeiva's favorable introduction to the exhibition catalog was replaced with Sergei Isakov's more critical essay. Although Ivanova preserved the proofs of the Anikieva essay,[4] she surely realized that the avant-garde would never officially be the art of the people.

According to Ivanova's son, Felix Ravdonikas, the artist was "devoted to the service of art"[5] and her work should be understood as a dialogue with the Russian people without immediate political motivations. Ivanova's own statements recorded in her diary reflect this sentiment inasmuch as Ivanova was, first and foremost, an artist: she felt duty bound to paint, and, with some exceptions, she painted in a style that could be accommodated within the ideology of Socialist Realism. In other words, Ivanova succeeded in adopting a style which was satisfying to her as an artist, but which did not counter the æsthetic demands of the Soviet cultural establishment.

Ivanova's work of the 1930s onwards is distinctive, more often than not owing little to the rhetoric of Socialist Realism. Furthermore, she produced rather few works devoted to such typical themes of the movement as the worker and the collective farmer; even those that she did produce reflected her individual interpretation. In *Worker in Factoryshop* (fig. 7, F35), despite its "relevant" subject, the heroism of the worker is downplayed, thanks in part to the Post-Impressionist style Ivanova has used to capture the moment. The image is contemplative, even lyrical, and would have appealed to a wide audience, even though, presumably, Ivanova did not intend to exhibit the work.

Ivanova directed much of her energy toward the depiction of the Russian landscape. One image in particular, *Farm Scene with Tractor* (fig. 8, F18), seems to bridge the gap between the occasional worker theme and the more frequent landscape imagery. This image shows an open landscape with a tractor driven by a farmer in the center of the canvas. Again, the viewer senses a contemplative mood as the worker goes quietly about his work—Ivanova's landscape paintings extend this tranquillity. *Church in Staraia Ladoga with Violet Reflection* (fig. 9, F27) presents the familiar Russian

2   Sheila Fitzpatrick, *Russian Revolution* (Ithaca, London: Cornell University Press, 1992), 122.
3   For a discussion of the Filonov episode at the RM, see Nicoletta Misler and John E. Bowlt, *Pavel Filonov: A Hero and His Fate* (Austin, TX: Silvergirl, 1983), 263-278.
4   Essay is currently housed in the Archive of the IMRC.
5   See Felix Ravdonikas, "My Mother, Liudmila Ivanova," in this catalog.

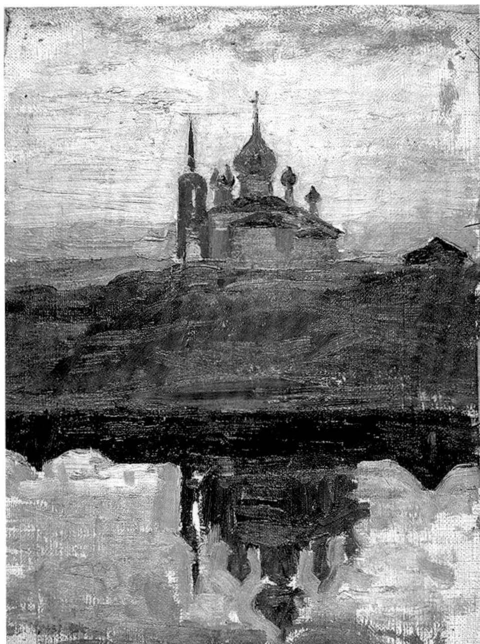

Fig. 9 Church in Staraia Ladoga with Violet Reflection (F27) 1948

architectural monument on top of a rolling hill reflected in a lake. Although Ivanova was not religious, her artistic interest in such a beautiful and serene image is easy to understand. In *Summer Landscape with Haystacks* (fig. 10, F38), we see, once again, an open landscape with large, pear-shaped stacks of hay. There is no trace of the worker or his machinery here, but rather, in addition to the beauty of the landscape itself, we see the task accomplished.

However, the shift in Ivanova's artistic evolution between the 1920s and the 1930s is not as clear-cut as it might seem. Of course, formally, the styles of Analytical Art and Socialist Realism differ vastly, but Ivanova seems to have explored each style in the conviction that, in creating an art for herself, she was also creating an art for the people. Initially, Ivanova subscribed to Filonov's doctrine of Analytical Art, but, when this avant-garde mode of communication fell into official disgrace, Ivanova—as a loyal Soviet citizen— focused her attention on other styles regarded as more accessible to the people. This was not a compromise to Ivanova; nor was the shift in artistic method unusual given external circumstances and her own personal beliefs.

In any case, the shift was not a clean break. In the early 1930s, for example, Ivanova moved between an almost Expressionist, Filonovian style (an Analytical portrait of 1931, has been described as a "symbol of grief at the death of her mother"[6]); moreover, she contributed to the collective illustrations in the Analytical style of

the 1933 Russian edition of the *Kalevala*.These illustrations attest that, like her more Realist work of the 1930s and 1940s, Ivanova's Analytical phase was a sincere effort to produce an art that would be acceptable to the proletariat public. Ivanova was not forced to change her style; rather, she accepted the system that rejected the avant-garde. When Realism became an integral part of the Party's cultural ideology, Ivanova chose to work realistically and to support the regime. Nonetheless, if she criticized the Analytical method, she did not denounce the inventor of that method.

Ivanova's art can help us to understand the special condition of early twentieth century Russian art as it relates to the cultural administration of political belief. In Ivanova's acceptance of, and adaptation to, the political realities of the Soviet Union we can appreciate the plight of an entire generation of artists who were nurtured in that political climate. The value of Ivanova art, then, lies not only in its reflection of an artist's personal psychology, but also in its description of the unique social and political reality in which she lived.

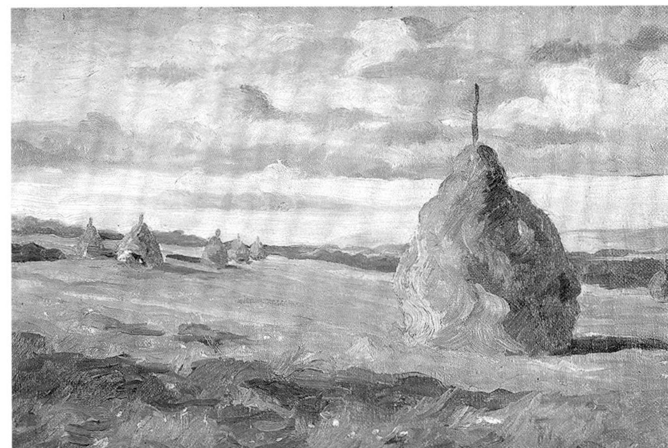

Fig. 10 Summer Landscape with Haystacks (F38) 1934-1950

6 Ibid.

What's in a Name? Titling the Untitled

ROMY M. VREELAND

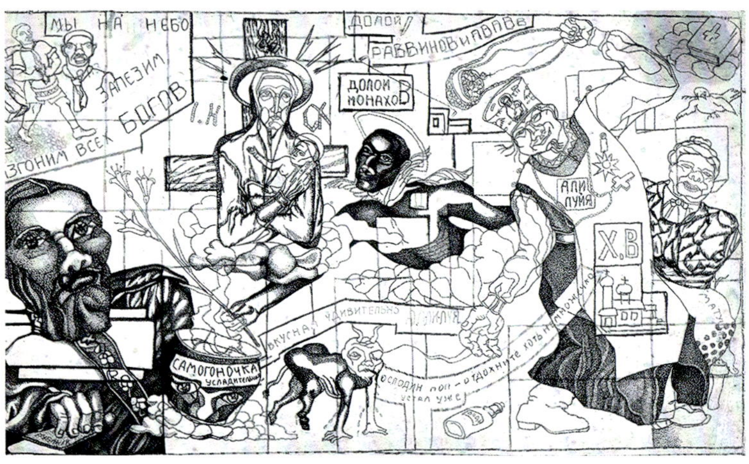

Fig. 11 Together We Will Climb Up to Heaven and Chase Out All the Gods (C37) 1925-1926

Labeling Liudmila Ivanova's works has been a challenging process, but the long debates over particularly difficult pieces reveal some of the basic problems that confront curators: What is the subject-matter of the work? Is it a figure study or a commercial design, or did it have some deeper ideological or political meaning? If none of these, should we ignore philosophical and thematic digressions and label the work purely on the basis of what we see? A more fundamental question occurred to us only later: Should we be labeling these works at all?

Early in our discussions, we realized that hanging countless works with such generic titles as "*Landscape #17*," "*Head B*" or, worse, "*Untitled*," would be both tedious and fruitless. For our own planning sessions, therefore, we concluded that labels which bore a direct relation to the subject-matter or composition of a work, rather than its registration number, would ease our task. In deciding upon titles, we devised the strategy according to which each title had to be (a) unique among the other works in the collection, (b) clearly descriptive of some defining feature in the work, such as the subject-matter or composition, (c) indicative of a thematic series within the collection (when applicable), and (d) free of external inferences as to the meaning of a work.

As we began to assign these labels, we found a section on titling works in W. McAllister Johnson's *Art History: Its Use and Abuse* especially valuable. Johnson divides the various titles born by works into two categories: "historical" (those which can be determined through examination of records such as bills of sale, the artist's correspondence, or exhibition catalogs) and "modern" (those which can be referenced through first-person accounts, i.e., through a contemporary artist or relevant art dealer). As Johnson stresses, however, few titles can be upheld as genuine as "all titles are of varying reliability, depending upon the epoch at which they appear or the care with which they were thought out"—even an artist's own title can be problematic.[1] For Johnson, however, the issue of a title's pedigree does not seem to be a major factor in determining whether a work should carry a title. A title given by someone other than the artist is not necessarily without merit since most works of art lack materially incorporated titles and must,

---

[1] W. McAllister Johnson, *Art History: Its Use and Abuse* (Toronto: University of Toronto Press, 1988), 304-305.

therefore, be assigned some identificatory name; such names should be purely analytical in nature and describe the major features of the work in question so as to "induce a mental set…useful to the art historian."[2]

Hazard Adams, a specialist in comparative literature, discounts approaches to titling like Johnson's, denying that major features of a work can be defined without subjective choice:[3] "Some properties are essential to some interpretations and inessential to others, but they are all simply parts of the work, and the true title [i.e., one given by its author] is one of these…. I hold that all titles are tropes belonging to artworks in the form of synecdoches."[4] Adams regards titles not given by the author as "labels, designators, and often interpretations, not merely guides to interpretation."[5] To support this conception of the term "title," Adams refers to the theorist John Fisher to illustrate that titles are not necessarily descriptions, even if they may contain descriptive elements. They are names not merely for the purpose of identification and designation, but for a uniquely hermeneutical—titles are names which function as guides to interpretation.[6] For Fisher, titles not only designate a work, but also facilitate its understanding, whether or not the artist has titled the work.

This view of titles, however, is problematic when titling untitled works, because it holds that any designation will affect a viewer's response to a work. Designating a work *Untitled*, for instance, may seem the height of objectivity, but it may incline the viewer to regard the work as secondary or subversive or even imply the artist's rejection (if only partial) of the work. Consider, too, an untitled work hanging among titled works at an exhibition: it functions without a verbal clue as to its meaning, so one might wonder why the artist chose to give the work no title. Was this intentional or was the title lost? Was the untitled work meant to be interpreted apart from the titled works and on a different level, like a commoner among counts and countesses?

Realizing that no effort on our part could be objective, we took to titling Ivanova's works with the collective voice of the curatorial team. Our titles cannot be "true titles" in Adams's sense, but they are able to facilitate discourse about the works. After all, it was precisely for this facilitative purpose that titling was made a standard practice in the academies of seventeenth and eighteenth century France and Britain. In order to submit a work to an annual salon or other juried show, a work needed both to be identifiable and to be easily placed in an accepted genre of painting. Clarity and adherence to æsthetic modes were the primary means of making a favorable impression with one's work.[7] Consequently, titles that challenged the viewer's interpretation of the subject-matter were avoided, while those that reinforced a reading of a work with say, an Arthurian legend as its subject, were favored.

As we progressed in our labeling of the Ivanova's works, we encountered a number of compositions which incorporated words. In titling these works, we found it helpful to consider the work of Stephan Bann on the titling of names in modern and post-modern art.[8] Bann adopts a semiotic approach that is concerned with the relation of various types of titles to the works to which they refer. Bann posits that a title functions as a legisign (a representational sign formulated in a common, public language) directly correlated to the painting's sinsign (a unique sign). In this way, the meaning of the legisign (title) is directly dependent upon the work itself.[9] Bann also points out, however, that titles evolve into sinsigns of their own as they become increasingly meshed with the works that they were once only meant to index, a process of transformation that began with the Cubists.

The indication that we are looking at a guitar or portrait of Ambroise Vollard supplies the indispensable prior orientation. Braque and Picasso give an increasing prominence to the stenciled or printed masthead—which detaches itself from the painted surface as a legible sign. In a work like Picasso's *La Bouteille de Pernod* (1912), the

2 Ibid., 213.
3 Hazard Adams, "Titles, Titling, and Entitlement To," *The Journal of Æsthetics and Art Criticism* 46, no. 1 (1987): 7-21
4 Ibid., 10.
5 Ibid., 12.
6 Ibid., 10.
7 Stephen Bann, "The Mythical Conception Is the Name: Titles and Names in Modern and Post-Modern Painting" *Word and Image* 1, no 2 (1984): 176-90.
8 Ibid.
9 Ibid., 172.

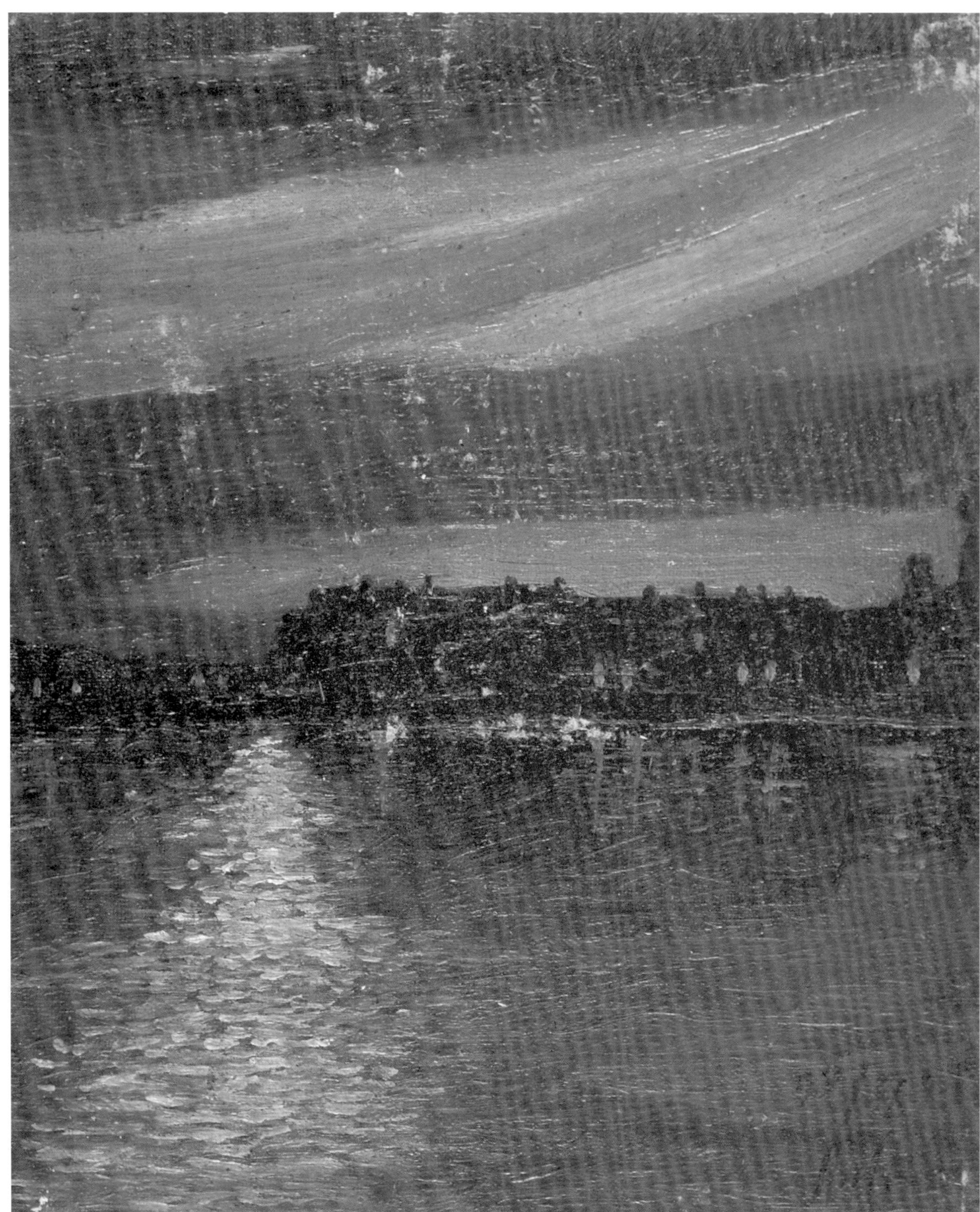

Fig. 12 Academy of Arts,
Petrograd, at Night (D4)
September 25, 1921

legisign of the title simply echoes the sinsign of Picasso's playfully inscribed bottle label.[10]

An analogous situation arose with Ivanova's *Together We Will Climb Up to Heaven and Chase Out All the Gods* (fig. 11, C37), words inscribed amidst the satirical figures of her drawing which we chose to serve as an appropriate legisign for the work itself. The design for *Congo Cigarettes* (fig. 36, E2) is another example of a title that incorporates a word extracted from the work, this time an advertisement. Though Bann regards the title as merely the echo of the original sign (the object itself), he draws a distinction between words within a painting and those extracted from it for use as a title. John Fisher, on the other hand, believed that words inscribed directly into the surface of a work must give the work its name—any other naming, even by the artist, could not be considered a true title; for Fisher, these words are to be used as a title in order to reinforce their function as "guides to interpretation."[11]

When compiling labels for Ivanova's works, we tried to avoid the jarring disjunctions of, for instance, Marcel Duchamp's *Fountain* (1918).[12] In fact, our titles really are no more than descriptive labels—and ones that can be changed at a later date just like any proper name. Whenever possible we tried to pull words from the compositions as identification tabs so that they would act as legisigns, not sinsigns.

A few works did inspire more technical language where we felt that a generic term might seem out of step with the innovative nature of a given image. For example, *Head: Sub-Dermal Detail* (C7) is a large composition in which a male's portrait has been drawn to reveal the musculature beneath the skin, but in a way very different from what might be found in an anatomy manual.[13] This sketch seems indebted to a pseudo-science, Filonovian, perhaps. The monstrous visage has one eye drawn in full detail that looks like a complex mechanical iris found in a camera. To have called this work simply *Study of a Head* or *Filonovian Head* would have been to ignore its unique and startling qualities. Another work, showing a series of lights reflected on a waterfront at night, was titled *Academy of Arts, Petrograd, at Night* (fig. 12, D4) because we have

documentary evidence that Ivanova's apartment faced the Academy across the Neva; this title exemplifies what Johnson (as well as Bann) would call an historical title, one derived from documentation by the artist and her son.

Titling the untitled is not a task to be undertaken lightly for it requires a broad knowledge of an artist's body of work and maximum information on the circumstances of his or her life. The labels that we have assigned Ivanova's paintings and drawings should be seen as temporary designations for they do not and cannot assume the artist's intention. Some of these labels may yet take on the status of accepted titles, but even if they do not, they will still have served their purpose in this exhibition and its concomitant literature.

10 Ibid., 182.
11 Adams, "Titles, Titling, and Entitlement To," 10.
12 See Bann, "The Mythical Conception Is the Name," 182-183.
13 *Head: Sub-dermal Detail*, C7, has not been definitively attributed to Ivanova.

Bringing Ivanova to Light: Restoration and Revelation

LINDA M. OH

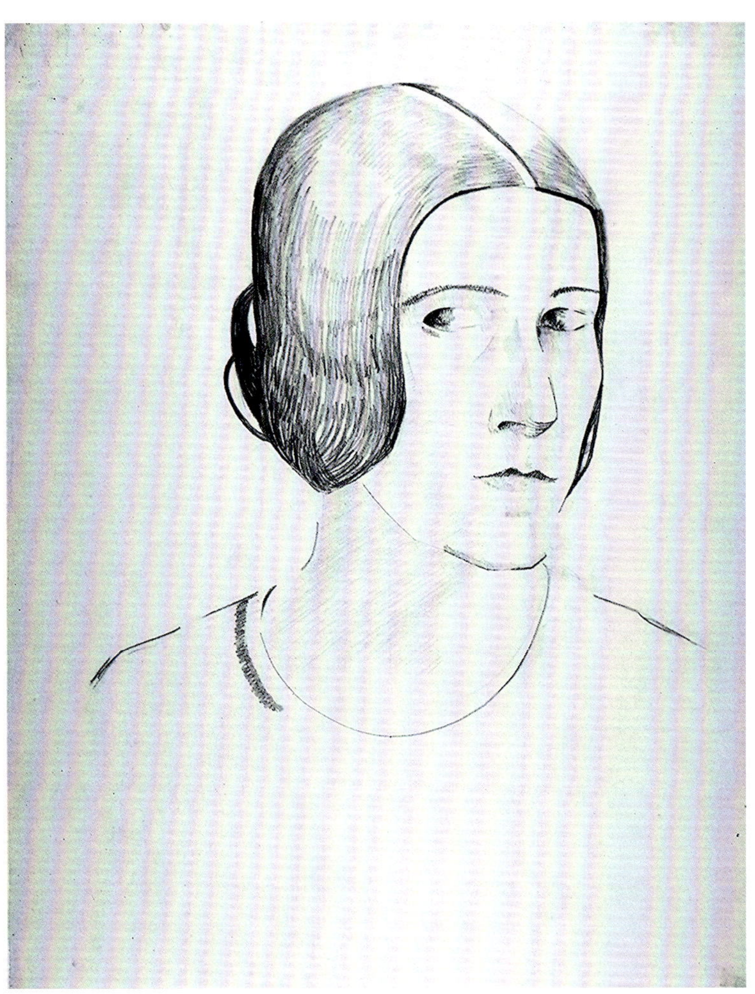

Fig. 13 Woman with Gaze Askance (B3) 1922, after treatment

"Myriad Thoughts, Myriad Desires: Liudmila Ivanova (1904-1977), An Artist in Soviet Russia" is the culmination to a spirited collaboration between the Museum Studies Program and the Institute of Modern Russian Culture (IMRC) at the University of Southern California, Los Angeles. The main purpose of this endeavor was to expose and assess a Russian artist whose talent had long gone unnoticed and to prevent the further deterioration of her artistic estate. With the encouragement of Ivanova's son, Felix Ravdonikas, the artist's family donated the estate to the IMRC in 1989, primarily in the hope that Ivanova's art and her contribution to the history of modern Russian culture would become better known. Our exhibition is a direct response to this concern.

The ultimate aim of our seminar and research, then, was to create the exhibition and its catalog, but, when first confronted with this task, we discovered that many of the more than two hundred objects in the bequest displayed some degree of damage. Indeed, forty-six major pieces, exemplifying Ivanova's rapid stylistic evolution, were in urgent need of care. The magnitude of the problem determined our immediate decision to favor discriminate restoration as a means of returning Ivanova's art to a sounder condition so that her *œuvre* would be preserved for posterity. On the other hand, Ivanova's drawings, pastels, watercolors, and oils had experienced—but had also survived—cataclysmic events such as the Nazi's blockade of Leningrad (1941-1943) as well as the common abuses of improper handling and storage, air pollution, humidity and temperature changes, and insect infestation. As far as we could ascertain, in almost seventy years preventive measures had never been taken to ensure the preservation and stability of Ivanova's works—the drawings, pastels, and watercolors had neither been matted nor properly stored (indeed, many had been stacked directly on top of one another without protective separations or dividers). A typical work like *Woman with Gaze Askance* (fig. 13, B3) had folds and creases in the paper and tears along the margins and corners. Likewise, no efforts had been made to shield the pictures' surfaces from abrasions while handling; nor were the works protected from the ravages sulphur dioxide and other pollutants entering from open windows and doors can inflict on works of art on paper.[1] Insect damage was also detected on the surfaces of many of the works

1   Francis W. Dolloff and Roy I. Perkinson, *How to Care for Works of Art on Paper* (Boston: Museum of Fine Arts, 1971), 22.0

(houseflies and cockroaches in particular are primary culprits who contribute to the staining and specking of paintings and drawings).

The conservation of works of art on paper presents special problems. The conservator must analyze the types of fibers in a particular paper as well as diagnose the deterioration problems and treat them. Hence, to help restore the collection to a semblance of its original condition, Linda Shaffer, a Los Angeles conservator of works of art on paper, was consulted regarding condition and possible treatment of *Woman with Gaze Askance*. According to Shaffer, this graphite drawing on commercial-weave paper was in extremely poor condition: there is—or was—severe discoloration, foxing (the red-brown, freckle-like staining of paper believed to be the result of chemical reactions between iron salts in the paper and organic acid released by fungi caused by humidity), cockling, crimps, and creases across the image (fig. 14).[2] Furthermore, Shaffer found heavy soiling from dust and dirt, water stains, two two-inch tears in the right margin, and abrasions and tears along the bottom resulting in losses of paper. The poor state of this drawing may be attributed to inadequate storage conditions or to placement in an undersized portfolio that left the margins of the sheet exposed to the environment.

The first procedure in the restorative treatment for *Woman with Gaze Askance* was to remove as much of the dust and dirt as possible by a surface dry cleaning. The severe discoloration and mildew (foxing) indicated that the paper contained acidic constituents that accelerate the decomposition of cellulose causing paper to become weak.[3] The paper was then tested for lignin, which was not detected. Lignin is a binding material present in wood, which if left untreated, breaks down into acidic components, giving paper an often undesired brown color.[4] Next, in order to soften the fibers, the drawing was humidified and soaked first in filtered, and then ammoniated, water. This procedure also permits the water to act as an effective wash by reducing the acidity in the paper and, thus, prolongs its longevity. Following, the drawing was bleached with a dilute deacidification solution, ultra-violet light, and with a dilute of buffered hydrogen peroxide, and then rinsed in filtered water. This procedure neutralizes the present acidity and leaves a sufficient protective residue to counteract acid for an extended period.[5]

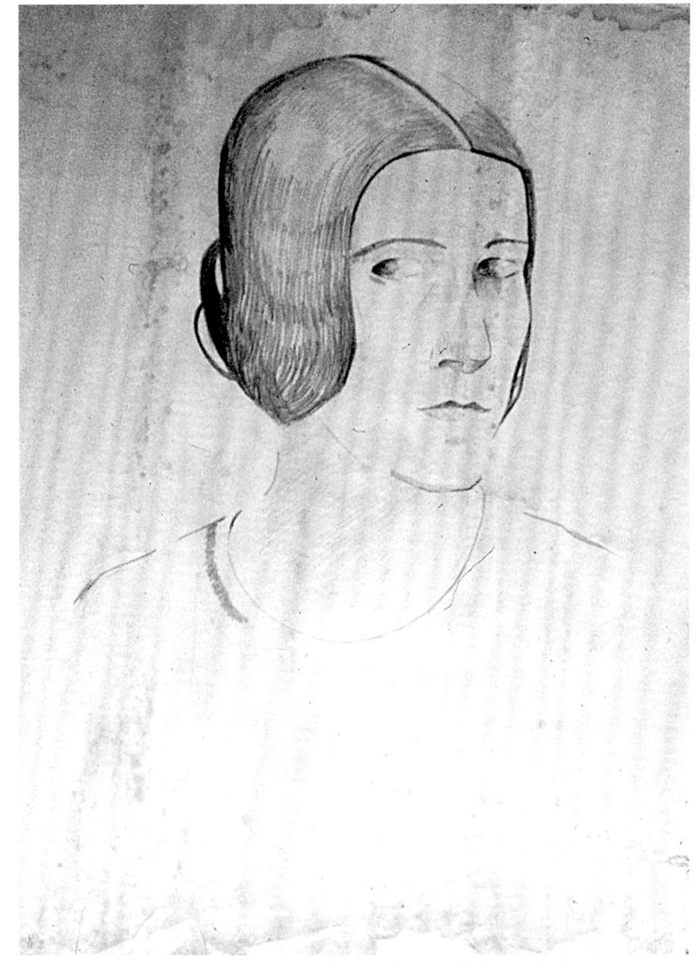

Fig. 14 Woman with Gaze Askance, (B3) 1922, before treatment

A closer look reveals crimps and creases pervading the vulnerable paper. The bottom margin is abraded and tears and losses occur along the periphery of the illustration. There is severe discoloration and two 2″ tears in the right margin. Like so many of Ivanova's works on paper, this drawing suffers from years of improper care.

2 Anne F. Clapp, *Curatorial Care of Works of Art on Paper* (Oberlin: Intermuseum Conservation Association, 1978), 36.
3 Hermann Kuhn, *Conservation and Restoration of Works of Art and Antiquities*, trans. Alexander Trone, 2 vols. (London: Robert Hartnoll, Ltd., 1986), 1:202.
4 Dolloff and Perkinson, 10.
5 Clapp, 18.

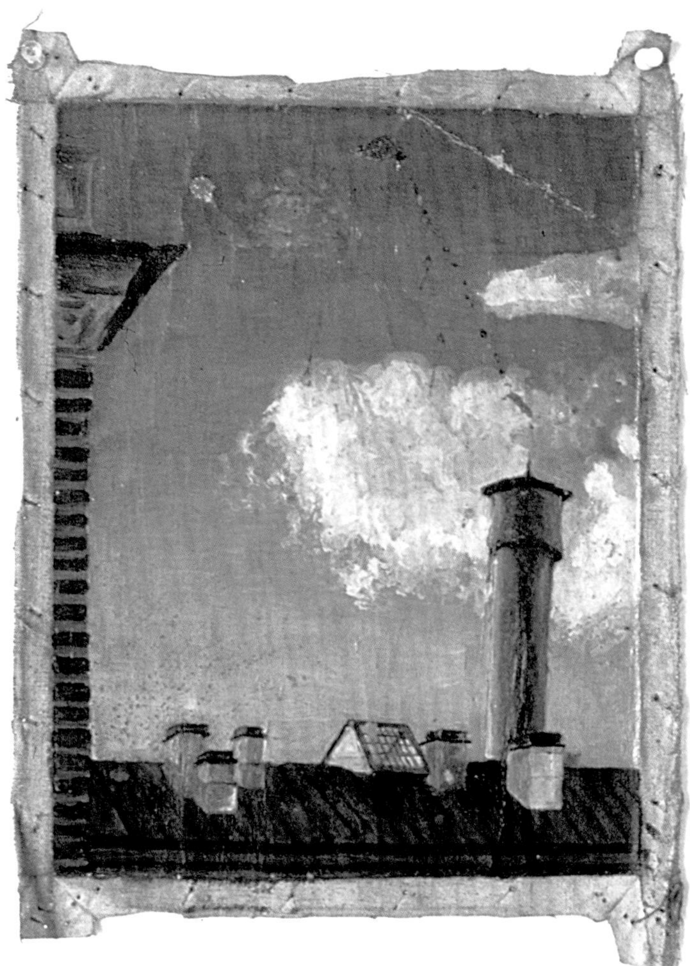

After the image was dried, the first stage of the bleaching process, including the rinse, was repeated. With the work in a damp state, the tears were then mended and the drawing was pressed in Hollytex with cotton blotters (a heavy blotting paper made of cotton) and weights in order to flatten it as much as possible. Owing to the scarcity of good quality paper (e.g., handmade rag paper) in the post-Revolutionary years, Ivanova was forced to use machine-made paper containing ground wood pulp and chemical additives whose inherent properties and impurities caused it to turn brown and become brittle and acidic.

Ivanova's paintings on canvas were also in dismal condition. Aside from the usual ravages of time, years of neglect exacerbated the damage. Most of the paintings had suffered from cracking along the folds and bends in the canvas caused by careless mishandling in addition to the damage caused by fluctuations in humidity evident in the loose grounds and paint layers. Of course, the longevity of a painting relies substantially on the quality of the support and, given the time and circumstances, it is unlikely that Ivanova or her contemporaries had ready access to good quality canvases. The availability of such material was so limited that Ivanova often reused the same canvas by painting over a preexisting image or by painting on the versos. Furthermore, none of the paintings received by the IMRC were fastened on stretchers, although some had tacking margins that indicated that they had once been stretched.

Aneta Zebala, a paintings' conservator based in Los Angeles, examined many of the oil paintings in the bequest, including *View of Rooftop Chimneys* (fig. 15, F43). In her condition report, Zebala noted that the painting was in poor visual and structural condition: a diagonal crease in the support (canvas) at the top right corner had caused cracking, flaking, and loss of paint, the numerous dark accretions on the surface included splattered mud in the upper region of the painting, and only the sky had been varnished. Though the painting was without a stretcher, it bore tack marks along the entire tacking margin. In order to stabilize the painting, loose or flaking paint was locally infused with appropriate adhesives. Then, the verso was surface dry cleaned with galvanized rubber sponges. Planar distortions were relaxed with minimal moisture and pressure on a suction table and a new, keyable stretcher was manufactured and assembled so that the painting could be restretched onto it. The painting was surface cleaned with an aqueous solution of a surfactant and the dark accretions were removed from the surface mechanically. The heavy crease along the right corner was alleviated by flattening the canvas on a suction table with the use of moisture and gentle heat. Next, the canvas was strip-lined (a procedure which fortifies the damaged or brittle edges of a canvas) both as a reinforcement of the fragile margins and as a safety precaution against any cracking or flaking of paint along the borders that might have occurred during the stretching process. Ultimately, losses and disfigurements were inpainted with suitable reversible paint. The term "inpainting" is used to refer to a conservator's restoration work in paint which is confined to the area of severe damage only. A painting of extraordinary, luminous beauty emerged from this restorative treatment (fig. 16).

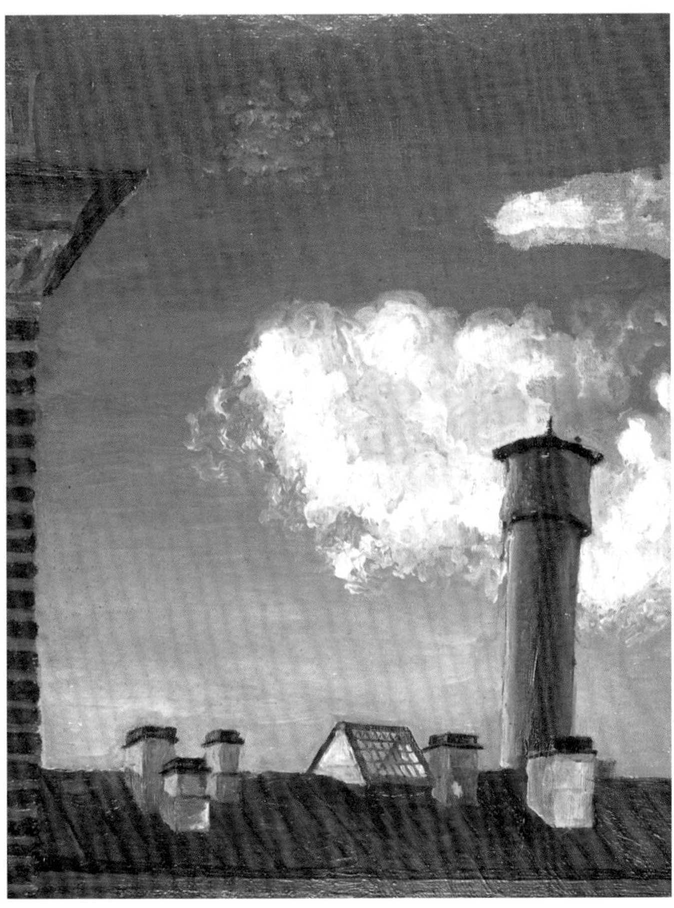

time (in the case of Ivanova, over seven decades), the canvas turns brittle, the ground (preparation applied to the support to render it more receptive to paint) detaches from the support (canvas), and the paint may crack, flake or change color, and accumulate grime and pollution. Excessive moisture makes paper become limp and develop mold while insufficient moisture causes paper to become fragile. When these changes become undesirably noticeable, deterioration is under way. Bad restorations can result in irreparable damage and every treatment or cleaning has potentially negative side effects if executed without due caution or discretion.[9] Nevertheless, intervention is necessary for an object to continue living and existing. Naturally, extreme care and attention were exercised in our submission of objects for their inaugural restoration and conservation treatment.

In cleaning, repairing, and revealing the works of Ivanova, we were forced to confront the basic issue of restoration and conservation, given the precarious state of the bequest. The Museum Studies Program and the IMRC made a unanimous decision not only to refurbish the appearance of Ivanova's art, but also, where possible, to prevent further deterioration. After cautious judgement, experts emphasized their intention not to deviate from the artist's original objective and, thus, in several of the restored objects, the missing sections of images were intentionally left blank. Each object was evaluated and considered independently; æsthetic decisions were based upon limitations set by the artist and by our exhibition budget. Ivanova used various media which were found to be soluble in water—hence the difficulty in performing any conservation treatment on those objects. However, fiber losses were filled along the edges of the drawings and minimal treatment was applied to stabilize the works. Images were not recreated or falsified to supplement the areas of loss in order to preserve the integrity and authenticity of the artworks.

To the historian and connoisseur Max Friedlander "restoration is a necessary evil."[6] In the preparation for "Myriad Thoughts, Myriad Desires" intervention was necessary, but the two conservators kept treatments to a minimum and undertook only non-invasive procedures. Their objective was to preserve the works by preventing or retarding deterioration and restore them to their creator's intent. As explained by Albert France-Lanord, "Restoration means to renew not only a material but a product of human activity. Whether it is a matter of works of art or simple objects, they are important not only because they are old or composed of matter but also because of all they hold that is still alive in them which, after the work of the excavator, we must bring to light."[7] Certainly, conservation techniques enable the viewer to appreciate what the artist had envisioned, while restoration merely recovers the property that the work once possessed—and possessed even in its deteriorated state.[8] Over

6 Max Friedlander, *On Art and Connoisseurship* (London: Bruno Cassirer, 1944), 267.

7 Albert France-Lanord, "Knowing How to 'Question' the Object Before Restoring It," in *Historical and Philosophical Issues in the Conservation of Cultural Heritage*, eds., Nicholas S. Price, K. Talley Jr., and Alessandra M. Vaccaro (Los Angeles: The Getty Conservation Institute, 1996), 245.

8 Anthony Savile, "The Rationale of Restoration," *Journal of Æsthetic and Art Criticism* 51, no. 3 (Summer 1993): 436.

9 James Beck, "A Bill of Rights for Works of Art," in *'Remove Not the Ancient Landmark': Public Monuments and Moral Values*, ed., Donald M. Reynolds (Amsterdam: Gordon and Breach Publishers, 1996), 71.

Restless Skies

NICOLETTA MISLER

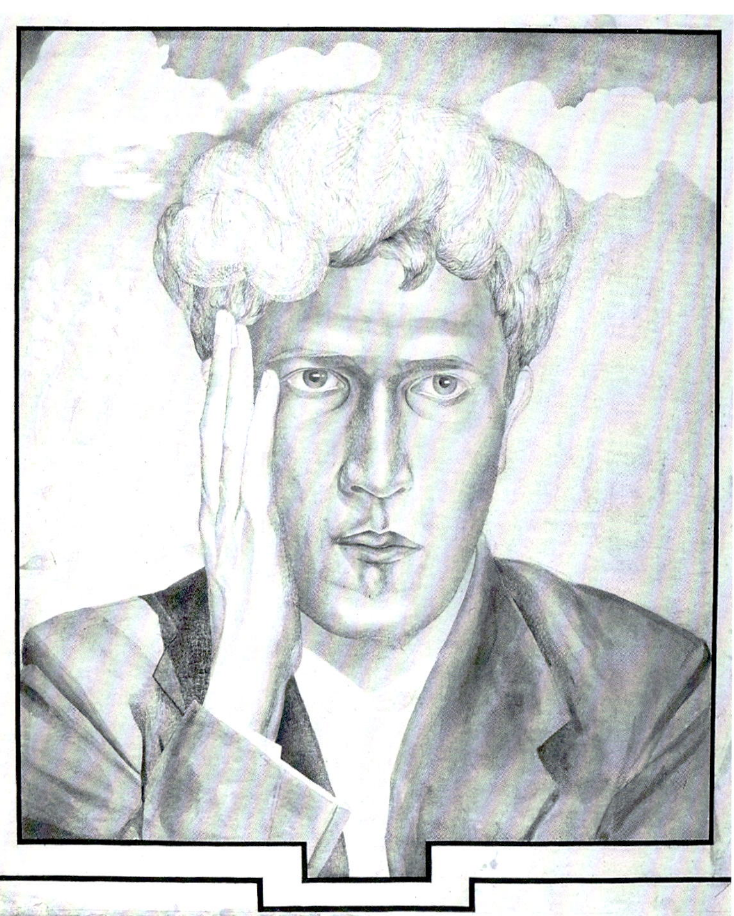

Fig. 17 Portrait of Man with Clouds (C12) 1925

In the numerous photographs, official passes, and identification cards that have come down to us, we see the face of Liudmila Ivanova; the face is soft, maternal, and sincere, but also self-willed and with the eyes she bequeathed her son, Felix Ravdonikas—ablaze and full of curiosity. In these fading photographs—some of which are included in "Myriad Thoughts, Myriad Desires"—we also see her hairstyle: severe, no-nonsense, parted unceremoniously down the middle and gathered at the back. Here is an icon of the true Soviet woman, genuine, straightforward, no hint of rhetoric: "I envy you your energy and *joie de vivre*" wrote her husband, Vladislav Ravdonikas, during the terrible years of the Second World War.[1] Here was a real *komsomolka* who, as she herself maintained, should not wear lipstick or dresses in the latest fashion like some bourgeois lady, should not use risqué language, and certainly should not bob her hair or wear pants.[2]

This kind of puritan Communist conformism should not surprise us when we remember that Ivanova's father and mother were members of the Communist Party, that, together with her second and third husbands, Nikolai Kuranov and Ravdonikas, she believed staunchly in the Communist cause, and that she did not hesitate to apply political axioms to her own creative work. As she exhorted herself, "Your palette and paint should be in battle formation."[3]

It is, however, more difficult to reconcile this severe outward image with the turbulence and unease of Ivanova's inner life, with the vagaries of her three husbands and five children, and with the many other passions—both intimate and artistic—that stirred her heart so young and so full. Unlike other celebrated women of the Russian avant-garde such as Natalia Goncharova and Liubov Popova, Ivanova comes to us in a portrait more synthetic, more authentic, and more alive, a portrait derived not only from the large corpus of works that have survived, but also from the vital testimony of her three sons and two daughters—something that renders Ivanova's character at once more distinctive and more elusive.

The paintings and drawings tell us that 1934 marked a key moment in Ivanova's complex evolution, just as she was passing from the influence of Pavel Filonov with all his primitive and exasperated

1 Vladislav Ravdonikas to Ivanova, Elaguba, 20 October 1942, call no. G94 (typescript materials concerning Ivanova's life), 93, Ivanova Archive, IMRC.

2 Manuscript leaves, Ivanova, "Gde komsomolizm (komsomoliia) konchaetsia i meshchanstvo nachinaetsia;" undated notebook, call no. G43, IMRC.

3 Ivanova to Ravdonikas, 13 September 1934, call no. G94, 52, IMRC.

intellectualism to a realistic and almost physical kind of painting—
and to the pleasure of painting in oil with its almost physiological
material density. For Ivanova, disengagement from Filonov signified
a return to representational art, whether practiced as a precise
instrument accompanying a scientific text, as the installation of an
exhibition, or as the copying of a mural. Even so, the ethical discipline of the artist's craft was still part and parcel of Filonov's pedagogical system, according to which the artist—whom Filonov called
the "master-researcher"[4]—was to learn his trade via the humble
copying of the Old Masters and even via rote craftsmanship (it is
surely not fortuitous that Ivanova made neat designs for cigarette
packs while Filonov did the same for candy wrappers). In any case,
Filonov also painted Realist—and Hyper-Realist—portraits and
almost photographic interiors, so Ivanova's censure of her mentor
from 1934 onwards would seem to concern the technique, not the
content or purpose of his oil paintings with their "Filonovian
mugs."[5] But if Filonov painted with such a velatura of subtle colors
that the surface is completely smooth and the image one of total
illusion, in her later landscapes, Ivanova used a heavy impasto,
rich, textured, and with clots of irregular paint—surely a program-
matic gesture. Incidentally, the often irregular and thick surface of
her canvases is one reason why some of her oils are in such poor
condition, brittle and fragile, with substantial paint loss.

Who was Pavel Nikolaevich Filonov (1883-1941) and why did his art
attract Ivanova—briefly, but intensely—while she was an aspiring
student in the mid-1920s? Antagonistic to such leaders of the
Russian avant-garde as Kazimir Malevich and Vladimir Tatlin,
Filonov believed in the prophetic mission and status of the artist—
and also in what he regarded as the democratic basis of the
painter's craft. To this end, he urged total dedication to the calling
of the artist, the cultivation of an impeccable technique, and the
aspiration to "Madeness" or "Analytical Art." To achieve the quality
of "madeness," Filonov a miniaturist technique whereby he
advanced from the tiniest section of the pictorial surface through
the pictorial space in accordance with a rigorous, internal, "mental
analysis." That is why Filonov left most of his works unfinished,

returning to a given work again and again; his omission of finite
titles and specific dates reflects a refusal to distance himself from
the artistic process. Filonov regarded both life and art as an endless
process whereby birth, growth, and death constituted an unending
cycle while composition and decomposition, evolution and revolution were ultimately the integrated parts of an organic whole: this
he describes as "Universal Flowering."

Unwaveringly loyal to his own artistic vision, Filonov led a life of
sensual denial (he is rumored to have lived on black bread and
strong tea, to have made his own shoes, and, in general, to have
lived virtually as a monk). But despite, or perhaps because of, his
exclusive devotion to the creative spirit, his obdurate promotion of
his system, and his polemical rejection of Cubism, Futurism, and
Constructivism, Filonov attracted many disciples, including Ivanova.
By the mid-1920s, he had become a living legend in the cultural
landscape of Leningrad. Ivanova was especially close to Filonov in
the mid- and late 1920s and a number of her works from that period
reflect his æsthetic ideas; by the early 1930s, however, she was
questioning and then criticizing his system as she turned to a more
concrete and realistic depiction of still-lifes and landscapes.

Indeed, Ivanova's paintings of the 1930s onwards demand of the
viewer a tactile and anti-intellectual perception: "The green trunks
of the spruces have become so warm and soft in color like velvet.
You want to rub yourself against them like a puppy and imagine
how nice that would be."[6] Not that Ivanova had become incapable
of attaining the spiritual transparencies of her mentor; for example,
Portrait of Man with Clouds (fig. 17, C12),with its microscopic
pointillist technique developed by the Filonov School, recalls
Filonov's own *Conqueror of the City* (fig. 18). Both portraits show a
hand in an unusual and mysterious gesture: in Ivanova's rendering,
it is fine and long (as in Filonov's), serving as a vertical support to
the cheek and lending a melancholy and meditative dimension
to the sitter. An absolute frontality dominates both portraits: these
strange individuals look within themselves and beyond the viewer,
one the conqueror of the sky, the other of the city.

4 N. Misler, "Pavel Filonov, Painter of Metamorphosis," in *Pavel Filonov: A Hero and His Fate*, eds. Misler and Bowlt
   (Austin, TX: Silvergirl, 1983). This was Filonov's definition of the artist who worked in the Analytical style, the true
   application of which canceled the differences between pupil and teacher: "The pupil is a master in the process of
   learning with all their rights and obligations of the master."
5 Ivanova's diary, 12 September 1934, call no. G94, IMRC. See also Felix Ravdonikas, "My Mother, Liudmila Ivanova,"
   in this catalog.
6 Ivanova's diary, 9 September 1934, call no. G87, 49, IMRC.

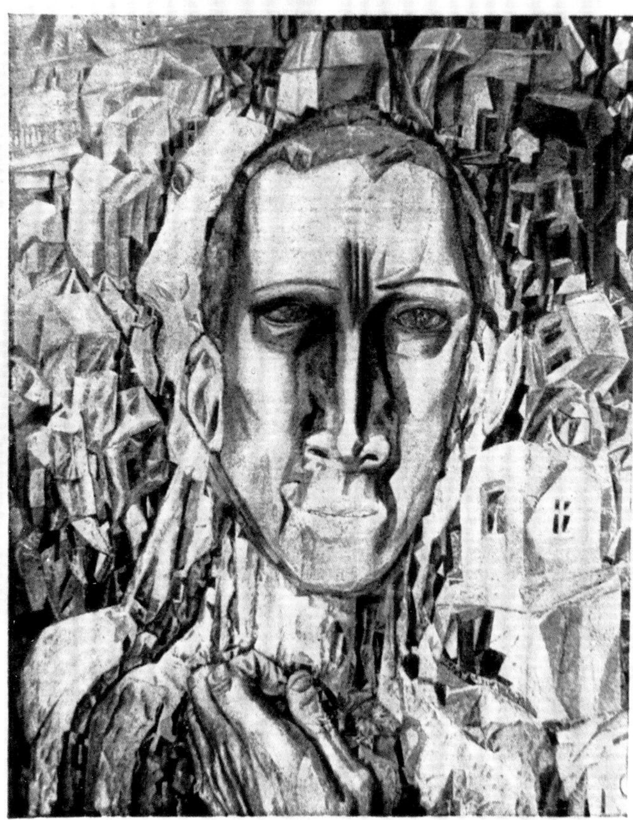

Fig. 18 Pavel Filonov, Conqueror of the City, 1914-1915, Russian Museum

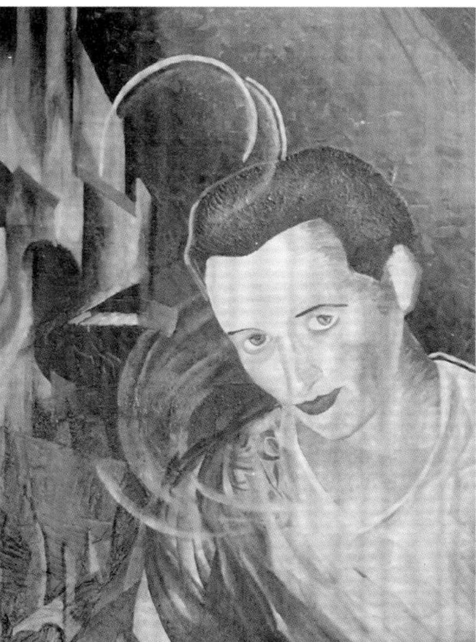

Fig. 19 Untitled Portrait
(of the artist's mother),
1931-1934,
oil on canvas,
Private Collection

The motifs of sky and clouds recur throughout Ivanova's artistic career and should be regarded as central to understanding those late landscapes totally devoid of human figures. Clearly, these landscapes represented a way for Ivanova to abstract herself from the weight and harshness of an everyday reality which she confronted with such courage and determination; they were her way of creating space for an interior vision. Indeed, we find the same kind of introspection in Ivanova's 1931 portrait of her mother (fig. 19). Painted just after her mother's death after a long battle with cancer, this portrait is at the same time, a gesture of liberation and distancing and of contemplation. In this sense, beyond any physiognomical coincidence, the portrait is also a self-portrait: the aura of diverse colors effusing from the head recalls not only the abstract and mystical behests of her mentors (above all, Filonov and Matiushin), but also a laical and concrete certitude of the inexplicability of death and the continued presence of loved ones even thereafter.

The diary entry for 12 September 1934 quoted by Felix Ravdonikas at the beginning of his introductory essay amply testifies to these intuitive and irrational (some might say "feminine") aspects. These two pages, almost luminous in their detail, reveal the sentimental and emotional character of our *komsomolka* yet they provide the analytical description of an unconscious psychological deprogramming from the guru Filonov and his sect, a kind of ritual de-initiation: "Convulsively I began to seek a way out and I found it. I took up that big canvas with its idiotic Filonovian mugs.... In a flash I had wiped it over with turpentine.... My hands trembling, I squeezed the paint out on to the canvas. This was altogether a moment of religious ritual."[7] Ivanova ends her outpouring with a detailed description of the tears of liberation that accompany the beginning of the new picture, her tears falling like a libation on to the canvas. Still, it should not be forgotten that Ivanova's second husband, Nikolai Kuranov, was also a disciple of Filonov and a cofounder of the Collective of Masters of Analytical Art,[8] also linked her to the Filonov School. In 1927, not without a hint of envy, Kuranov writes to his wife: "You even find time to visit libraries and [various] organizations and drop by Filonov, too."[9] But Ivanova's release from the "nightmare" of Filonov[10] and her sigh of relief are also a sublimation—and metaphor—of her separation from Kuranov and his custody of their son, Yurii. The episode was no less traumatic and guilt-ridden than her separation from Filonov, as witnessed by her intense correspondence with Kuranov.[11]

7 Ivanova's diary, 12 September 1934, call no. G94, 51, IMRC.
8 In his essay "Iz istorii russkikh khudozhestvennykh gruppirovok, Obedinenie "kollektiv Masterov analiticheskogo iskusstva (Shkola Filonova)," Pavel Efimov contends that Kuranov and Trukhachev helped found the Collective, but did not play an active role in the subsequent life of the group, typescript from 1988, 7, IMRC.
9 N. Kuranov to Ivanova, 13 April 1927, call no. G94, 33, IMRC.
10 Ivanova's diary, 12 September 1934, call no. G94, 51, IMRC.

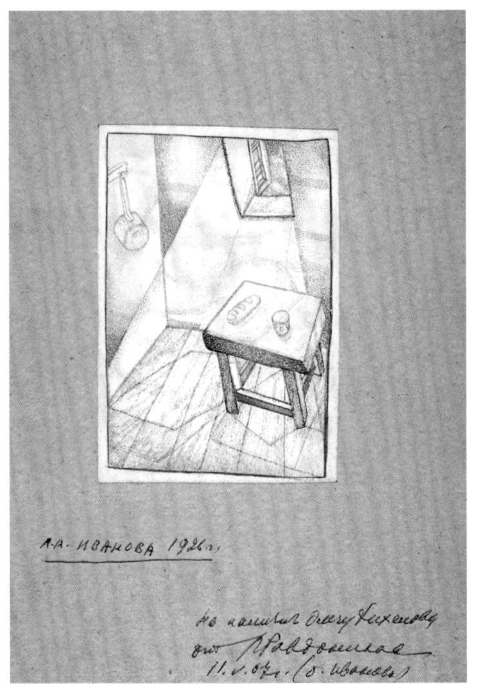

Fig. 20 Kitchen Scene
(C27) 1926

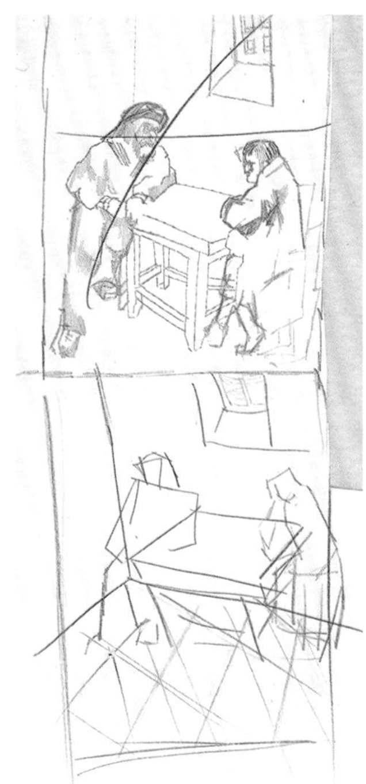

Fig. 21 Studies for Kitchen Scene
(C42) 1926

The young Ivanova seems to have joined the Filonov circle just as the Collective was forming in 1924-1925 (her earliest Filonovian works date to 1925), when students at the Academy of Arts came together in the Academy studio that Filonov was allowed to use (June 1925 onwards) and then at his apartment. Ivanova's early papers, especially a green exercise-book, contain notes that she and her colleagues took while studying at the Academy,[12] including two of Filonov's theoretical documents of the 1920s[13] and even "Made Paintings"—the first manifesto that Filonov and his immediate colleagues issued in 1914.[14] The fact that they all bear Kuranov's signature indicates that he had copied them scrupulously and then given them to Ivanova as was wont among Filonov's pupils. In other words, personal feelings played an important role in her involvement in, and subsequent rejection of, the Filonov School. Another cofounder of the Collective was Alexander Trukhachev, at first Kuranov's friend and then a turncoat informant—another of those piquant morsels in the tragic mix of private destinies under Stalin.[15]

Among the very few Analytical works that Ivanova signed and dated is the 1926 watercolor *Kitchen Scene* (fig. 20, C27), for which there exist two preparatory drawings on a single sheet of paper (fig. 21, C42). All three pieces demonstrate how Ivanova was already processing and manipulating Filonov's language: if the tiny dotted colors (*à la Filonov*) lend a corpuscular physicality to the light, the perspective is altered through three progressive phases, each one drawing attention to the half window, the narrow opening through which light flows into the room. The first preliminary sketch with its stone table and almost correct linear perspective has been crossed out—yet it bears the closest resemblance to Filonov's work (cf. *Pub,* 1924, fig. 22, present whereabouts unknown).[16] The second sketch multiplies the vanishing points downwards, toward the center of the room, whereas the finished watercolor causes the light to reflect and refract on the floor as it plays with the complex perspective. Filonov's claustrophobic interiors, charged with gloom, have given way to a room of serenity, inundated by light—a Dutch interior bereft of people, but full of pure light and space. But Architectural Interior still bears witness to Filonov's "madeness."

The watercolor *Four Objects with Cryptic Writing* (fig. 23, C38), Ivanova's second dated Analytical work, carries a double date

11 Ivanova to Kuranov, c.1927, call no. G94, IMRC. In this letter that Ivanova sent her ex-husband (who sent it back) she alludes to a suicide attempt.

12 Notebook, nd., call no. G3, IMRC.

13 Ibid., "Doklad Filonova v metodicheskoi chasti" (23.V.1925), 18 (verso) -25. "Filonov do revoliutsii (1910 gg.). Intimnaia masterskaia zhivopistsev i risovalshchikov. Sdelannaye kartiny," 26-27; "Osnova prepodovaniia izo brazitelnogo iskusstva po printsipu chistogo analiza kak vysshaia shkola tvorchestva," 28-32 (signed and dated "Kuranov, 7/VI/ 1925, midnight"). Notebook, nd., call no. G6, IMRC is another manuscript version of the latter. For an English translation and discussion, see Misler and Bowlt, *Pavel Filonov*, 155-165.

14 For an English translation and discussion of this manifesto, see Misler and Bowlt, Pavel Filonov, 135-38 [Bibl.].

15 Kuranov to Ivanova, 1955, call no. G94, 47, IMRC. Kuranov relates the episode to Ivanova asking for a letter of recommendation to support his rehabilitation; in this letter, Kuranov declares himself to be a Communist.

16 The Ivanova Archive contains an academic album (from after 1902) full of elaborate perspectival drawings— indicating her strong interest in academic perspective, anatomy, and proportion. call no. A1-21, IMRC.

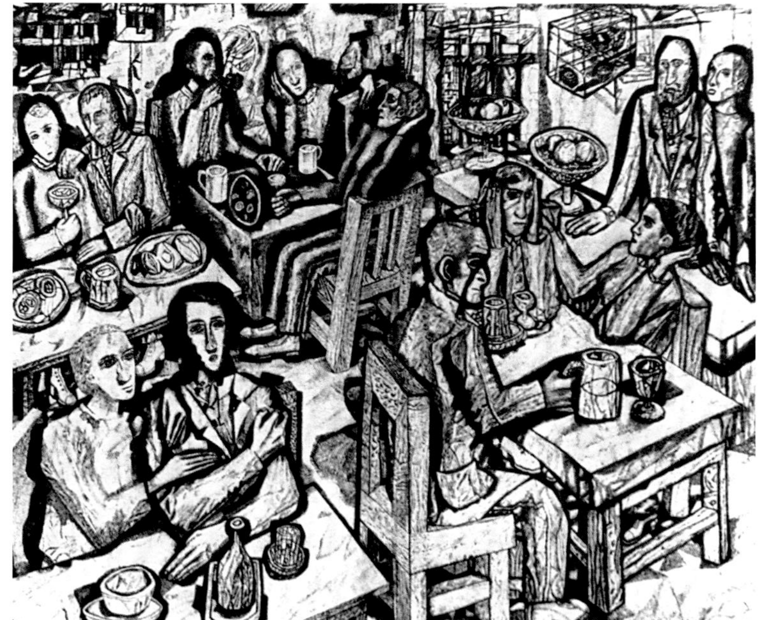

Fig. 22 Pavel Filonov, Pub, 1924, whereabouts unknown

Fig. 23 Four Objects with Cryptic Writing (C38) July 1925-January 1927

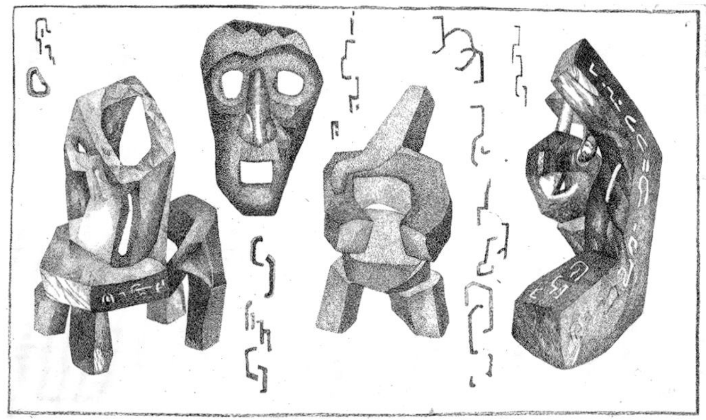

Fig. 25 Pavel Filonov, Hooligans 1923-1924, Russian Museum

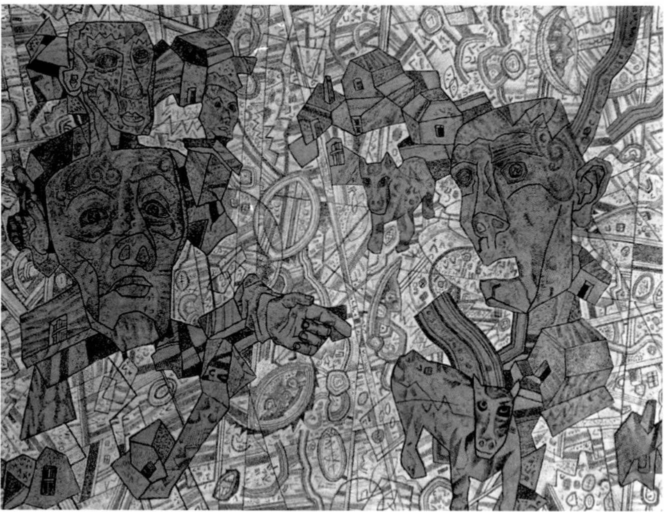

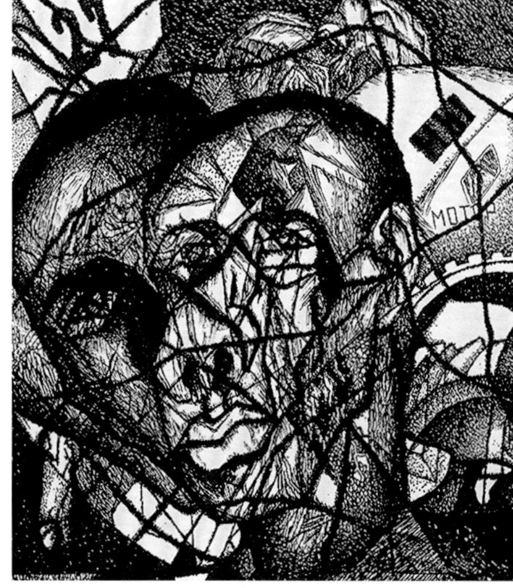

Fig. 24
27:Heads
(C36) 1925

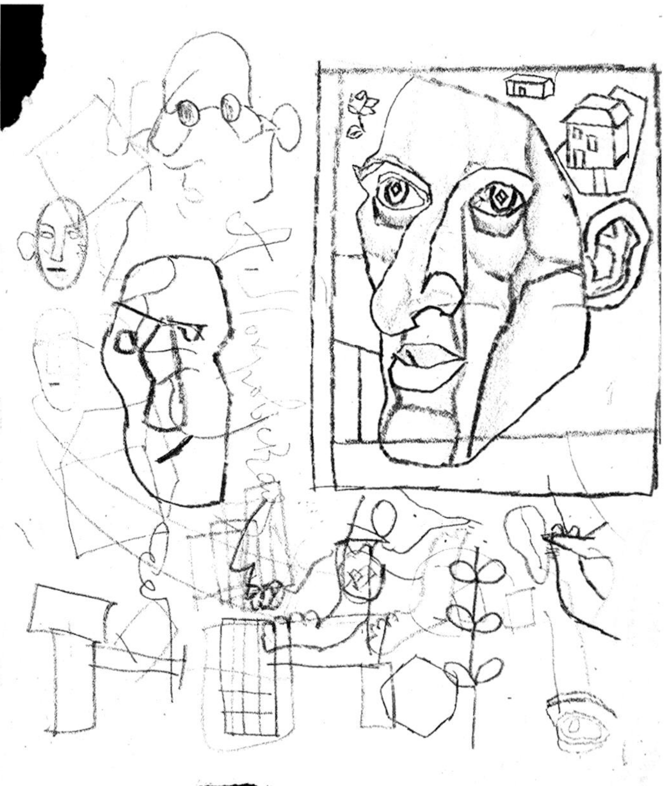

Fig. 26 Free Hand Sketches of Faces (C17) 1924

"begun July 1925 finished January 1927," a chronological elonga-
tion typical of Filonov. This powerful surface, with its rendering of
stone sculptures and a stone mask blindly looking at the viewer, is
painted with the tiniest brushstrokes. Here are "non-objects" full of
holes, located in a "non-space" as if from another planet; in fact,
the elegant, translucent touch of paint—light mauve—contradicts
the faceted structure of the heavy stone in which even the veining
has been traced. The writing in the picture alludes to the intricate
and articulated kind of cryptic non-alphabet that Filonov used in his
painting and that elicited attention and bewilderment of his viewers
(perhaps another reason for describing Filonov as a sectarian). The
concentration and mysterious resonance in the rather slight *Four
Objects and Cryptic Writing* may be a preface to Ivanova's subsequent
illustrations of and more pragmatic interest in archaeological relics.

A third drawing, *27: Heads* (fig. 24, C36), perhaps the most typical
of the Filonovian series, also dates to 1925 (presumably the date
the work was begun; the "27" inscribed in the upper-left corner
seems to refer to its completion). In *27: Heads*, repeating one of the
few key subjects that Filonov explored in the mid-1920s, Ivanova
interprets two "urban" dwellers from the lower classes (bald heads
and gross physiognomies) that recall Filonov's drawing *Hooligans*
(fig. 25) and *Two Heads* (undated, RM). Irregular lines divide the space
into triangles, a device that Ivanova applies in almost all her Filonovian
drawings as a private interpretation of the fragmented and discon-
nected space of Filonov's own vision.

Among other Filonovian elements to be found in Ivanova's work of
the mid-1920s is a passive reception of his particular thematic
motifs and formal devices. This is especially clear from pencil pieces
such as the double-sided *Freehand Sketches of Faces* (fig. 26, C17)—
an ABC of the Filonov iconology with the sad profile and a large
nose, the enormous ear, the square framing of each image, the big,
open nostrils (from below they look like the nostrils of some wild
beast), and even the tiny signs resembling an alphabet. So close is
the association with Filonov that the immediate impression is that
these heads may have been one of his own pedagogical exercises.

Ivanova's way of working on the paper also brings Filonov's pedagogical method to mind. Using short, precise strokes of a very
sharp pencil, she created a basic skeleton to which she lightly
applied a very fine brush, like the nib of a pen. Viewed from the
verso, the drawing may appear "incised" into the paper. According
to Filonov, colors were supposed to be applied only after this procedure had been followed—at which point the artist could carry on
and complete the process until "madeness" had been reached.

For this reason, some of Ivanova's works on paper seem to be colored randomly and arbitrarily.

One group of Ivanova's images, the propagandistic pieces, also
draws on Filonov's vocabulary for they are charged with political
invectives against religion, colonialism, and female exploitation
(prostitution). But, as in analogous works by other members of the
Filonov School, Ivanova's interpretations prove to be a chaotic
mix of messages, iconographies, and styles.

Ivanova's last gesture to the Filonov system was her participation in
the collective illustrations for the Russian edition of the Finnish
epos *Kalevala* (published in 1933). In 1932, the Party Decree "On
the Reconstruction of Literary and Artistic Organizations" terminat-
ed the Collective of Masters of Analytic Art, along with all other
artistic groups, although a split in the Collective had previously
occurred in 1930. An anonymous notebook on the *Kalevala* and
Filonov in the Ivanova refers to the Decree,[17] and repeats the censo-
rious clichés that the conservative critic Serge Isakov forged in his
introduction to the catalog of the Filonov one-man exhibition at the
Russian Museum in 1929.[18] What was Ivanova's position? Could she
have penned these negative remarks on the *Kalevala* or did she
simply keep them as evidence of the vicious campaign against
Filonov? As we learn from the memoirs of Felix Ravdonikas, Ivanova
never wavered in her respect for Filonov—and preserved not only a
first draft of the Isakov's negative introduction (heavily underlined
in the most ideological sections), but also the first proofs of the
original, sympathetic essay by Vera Anikieva (with Filonov's annota-
tion) which was excised and replaced by Isakov's.[19] The Ivanova
archive preserves another (unsigned, but probably by Anikieva) text
(in typescript and manuscript) for the catalog of an exhibition of
Petr Konchalovsky's works at the Russian Museum.[20] The fact that
Ivanova was a research assistant at the Russian Museum in those
same years (1928-1930) might explain how these items came into
her possession, although this does not explain why she kept
them for so long.

A victim of complex personal events (a new marriage, new children)
and tragic social events (the Second World War, The Leningrad
Blockade, evacuation, the arrest and release of her husbands, the
disappearance of her firstborn), Ivanova was unable—or unwilling—
to choose between the loyalty demanded by the Party apparatus
and a compassionate loyalty to her strongest mentor: after all, it was
Filonov who taught that the loftiest value for an artist is an inex-
orable belief in the inner vision. Ivanova never doubted this demand.

17 Anonymous notebook on the *Kalevala* and Filonov, nd., call no. G78, IMRC.
18 S. Isakov, untitled essay in *Filonov*, ex. cat. (RM; 1930), 3-28.
19 Anikieva was an intelligent art critic arrested in 1937; for an English translation and discussion of Anikieva's essay,
   see Misler and Bowlt, *Pavel Filonov*, 53-68.
20 V. Anikieva (?), undated typescript, call no. G42; and undated manuscript page (draft), call no. G38, IMRC.

"A Certainty of Eye and Hand": Ivanova and Petrov-Vodkin

DAVID BORGMEYER

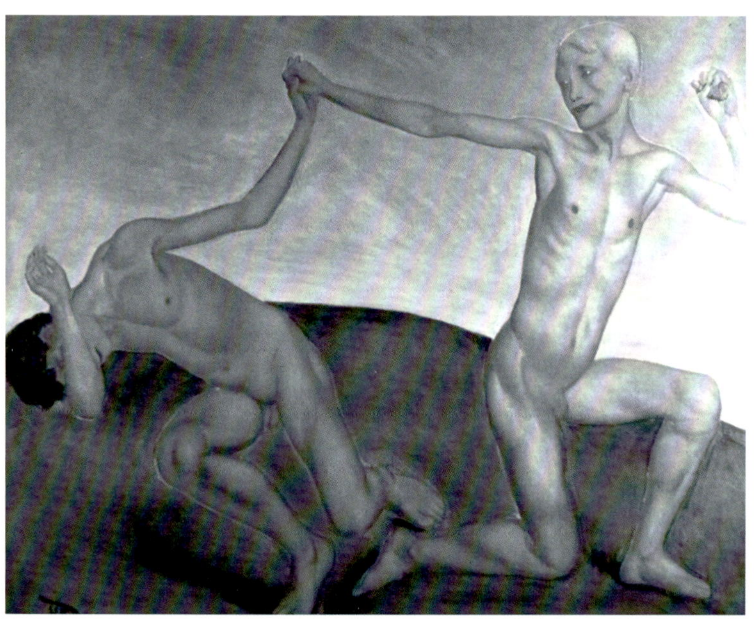

Fig. 27 Kuzma Petrov-Vodkin, Boys Playing, 1910-1911, oil on canvas, 123 x 157 cm, Russian Museum

While a student at the Academy of Arts between 1921 and 1926, Ivanova noted down a theory of color under the title "On the Laws of Color."[1] The correlation between Ivanova's own observations and those of Kuzma Sergeevich Petrov-Vodkin (1878-1939) are by no means coincidental:

Ivanova: "Color is the attribute of all objects that reflects certain rays, detaining all other rays. Yellow objects reflect yellow rays, absorb all blue and red, red objects reflect all red rays, etc."[2] Petrov-Vodkin: "We see a red object, but what does that mean? It means, that the object does not receive and reflects all red rays and absorbs blue and yellow."[3]

Ivanova: "[Yellow, red, and blue] each have complements made up of the combination of the other two: violet, green, and orange. In other words, each of the three are compound [*sostavnykh*] colors."[4] Petrov-Vodkin: "Intermediate colors: violet, green, and orange are compound colors [*sostavnymi*]. They mix in themselves a pair of primaries."[5]

It cannot be doubted that Petrov-Vodkin influenced Ivanova's artistic development. Petrov-Vodkin had a profound impact on the artistic curriculum at the Academy of Arts, culminating in the acceptance of his pedagogical plan in the mid-1920s as a standard part of the overall curriculum. Other than courses in Soviet ideology, all the courses listed on Ivanova's transcripts are to be found in Petrov-Vodkin's program for the Academy's painting department—the same department in which Ivanova was enrolled.[6] But who was Petrov-Vodkin? What was Petrov-Vodkin's system of art and art pedagogy and how does his influence manifest itself in Ivanova's work?[7]

1 Ivanova diary, 10 September 1934, call no. G94, IMRC.
2 Notebook, Ivanova, n.d., call no. G3, Ivanova Archive, IMRC. All translations are the author's.
3 Yurii Rusakov, ed., *Kuzma Sergeevich Petrov-Vodkin.* "Khlynovsk, Prostranstvo Evklida, Samarkandiia" (Leningrad: Iskusstvo, 1982), 498.
4 Notebook, nd., call no. G3, IMRC.
5 Rusakov, *Kuzma Sergeevich Petrov-Vodkin*, 498.
6 Svidetelstvo (diploma/transcript), nd., call no. G30, IMRC. The list of courses completed between 1921 and 1926 includes perspective, projection drawing, physics, optics, chemistry, anatomy, technology of painting materials, history of Russian art, history of the revolutionary movement, political economics, historical materialism, state-building of the USSR, basic painting, general drawing, and departmental drawing; foreign languages are not included.
7 Most published material on Petrov-Vodkin is in Russian. In English, see Tamara Machmut-Jhashi, "The Art of Kuzma Petrov-Vodkin 1878-1939" (Ph.D. diss., Indiana University, 1995); Kirill Sokolov, "Extracts from Euclidean Space, the Book by K.S. Petrov-Vodkin (1878-1939)," *Leonardo* 11 (Spring 1978), 140-44; In French, see Xenia Muratova, "Kouzma Petrov-Vodkine en Bretagne" in *Bretagne: art, création, société: en l'honneur de Denise Delouche*, Xenia Muratova et al. (Rennes: University Press of Rennes, 1997), 81-90.

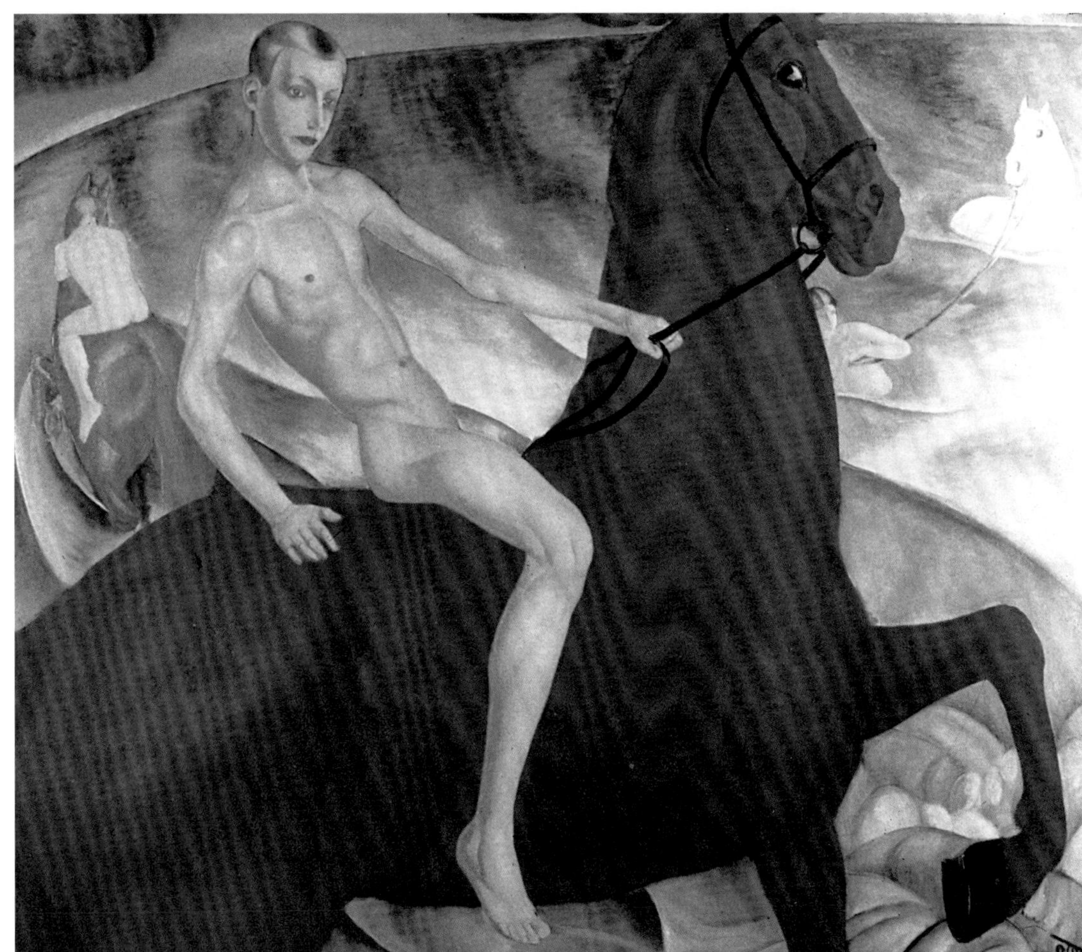

Fig. 28
Kuzma Petrov-Vodkin,
Bathing of the Red Horse,
1912, oil on canvas,
160 x 186 cm,
Tretiakov Gallery

Petrov-Vodkin transfered his allegiance to the new proletarian state after the October Revolution of 1917, and, like many non-academic artists of the older generation, found his way into the state teaching system.[8] He became a professor at the successor institutions to the Imperial Academy of Arts, where Ivanova studied from 1921 to September 1926. Petrov-Vodkin first trained under an Old-Believer icon painter and then at the Moscow Institute of Painting, Sculpture, and Architecture, which he graduated in 1905, before studying in Europe and North Africa for three years. Around 1910, he shifted from a conservative Symbolism and a muted palette to a spiritual monumentalism with distinctive volumetric modeling in vibrant colors, drawing heavily on the art of old Russian icons—as in *Boys Playing* (fig. 27) and *Bathing of the Red Horse* (fig. 28), his most celebrated canvas. Such works coincided with Petrov-Vodkin's elabora-tion of his own artistic and pedagogical theories—a theory of form and color that he called *trekhtsvetie*, a "three-color" system based on a particular application of blue, yellow, and red, integrated with a theory of space that he came to call *planitarnost* or "planetarity."[9]

Despite the small number of works in colored media surviving from Ivanova's student years, several images indicate practical connections between Ivanova and Petrov-Vodkin. For example, *Still Life with Bread and Butter* (fig. 5, F47, p. 28) directly imitates Petrov-Vodkin's style, composition, and palette as exemplified in *Grapes* (fig. 29). Another relevant piece is the large human figure from Ivanova's Academy years, *Boy in Black Trunks* (D1):[10] the tones are not as intense as those in many of Petrov-Vodkin's oils,[11] but, by retaining the integrity of local areas of color at the expense of

8 As in the case of Ivanova, Petrov-Vodkin's relationship with the Soviet state was ambiguous, in spite of the efforts of Soviet scholars to regard the October Revolution as the watershed of his career.

9 Petrov-Vodkin's theories would seem to share common elements with the color theories of Vasilii Kandinsky and Mikhail Matiushin (another of Ivanova's teachers).

10 Felix Ravdonikas suggests that this work dates from the mid-1930s, although the mid-1920s would seem to be more feasible. See Ravdonikas, *Priznaki zhizni khudozhnika. K 95-letiiu Liudmily Ivanovoi* (St. Petersburg: Ravdonikas, 1998). For portions of this essay, see Ravdonikas, "My Mother, Liudmila Ivanova," in this catalog. The full text (original typescript and xerox publication in ten copies) is housed in the Archive of the IMRC.

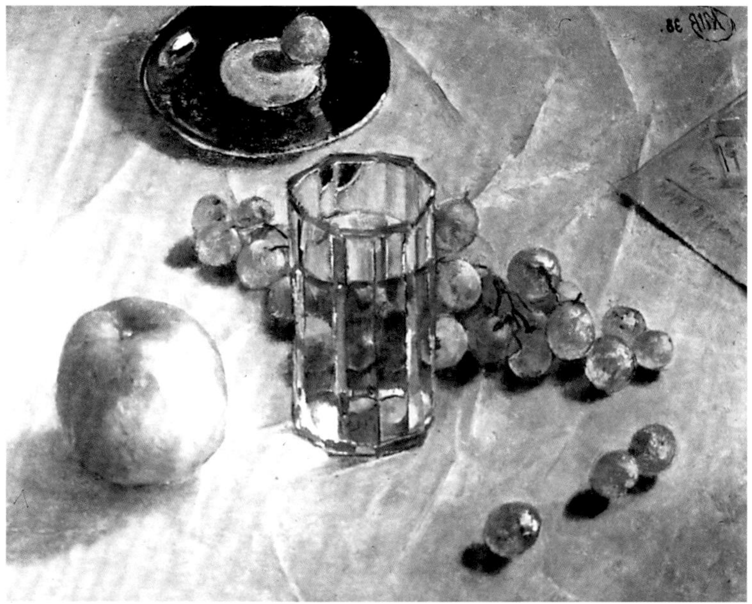

Fig. 29 Kuzma Petrov-Vodkin, Grapes, 1938,
oil on canvas, 37,3 x 48 cm,
Russian Museum

abstract to the concrete, multisided, and whole."[15] For Petrov-Vodkin, there were three basic tasks: first, line as the border of several planes; second, line as [creating volume]; third, to combine the two.

Ivanova's Academy drawings such as *Woman with Gaze Askance* (fig. 13, B3, p. 36) (a common motif in Petrov-Vodkin's œuvre) and *Seated Figure with Hand on Knee* (B1), probably of 1922, reflect his philosophy. In both works, the character of the line is determined by the function of the line within the composition, creating either a planar border or volume. *Woman with Gaze Askance* has close thematic and compositional links with Petrov-Vodkin's painting, especially in the rendering of line, the fusion of the brow and nose as a single plane, and the description of the contours of the eye, upper cheek, and lip. Petrov-Vodkin may well have derived this modeling of the head from Russian icon painting. Whatever its source, Ivanova repeats the device.

The same technique of using two distinct types of line, one to outline planes and another to give them volume, is at work to a much greater degree of refinement in Ivanova's *Standing Female Nude: Three-Quarter View* (B4). This application of a multiplicity of planes to describe volumetric form may have come to Ivanova through Petrov-Vodkin from Mikhail Vrubel, who was an important source for Petrov-Vodkin's early career. In any case, the standing nude shows full command of the technique. In the academic *Back View of Nude with Bent Left Knee* (B12) and *Man with Parted Hair* (B10), the description of separate planes has entirely disappeared. The rendering of volume in *Back View of Nude* is strongly reminiscent of the deep tonal shifts in Petrov-Vodkin's oil paintings such as *Boys Playing*.

As with the theories of color and line, Petrov-Vodkin's original theory of representing space is also manifest in Ivanova's work.[16] What Petrov-Vodkin called *mirnoe prostranstvo*, "world space," expressing his notion of the cosmic or of "*planitarnost*," has been been analyzed as:

naturalism, Ivanova remained loyal to Petrov-Vodkin's injunction against "mixing colors on the canvas as the Impressionists used to do."[12] Similarly, Ivanova's Filonovian rendering of the *Crucifixion with Pioneer Boy* (fig. 41, C23, p. 59) and her pastel on paper called *Four Figures on a Blue Background*[13] (fig. 39, B13, p. 58)carry a bright blue background borrowed directly from Petrov-Vodkin's religious compositions, the most outstanding example of which is *Virgin of Lovingkindness* (fig. 30).[14] Similar to the red backgrounds of the Novgorod icons that he valued so highly, the blue background invests his work with a deep spiritual quality. Though Ivanova's pastels lack the spiritual power of Petrov-Vodkin's canvases, the source of the blue background is his.

Assessing Ivanova's achievements as a painter at the Academy from the works in the IMRC collection is difficult, but the much larger number of works in pencil and ink on paper from this period provide us with a sense of her early drafting abilities. Here as well Petrov-Vodkin's influence is in strong evidence. Petrov-Vodkin recognized that the "proper beginning for the study of art was familiarity with paper and pencil, from plane to line, only gradually moving from the

---

11 The handling of volume is very close to the graphic work *Standing Female Nude: Three-Quarter View* (also reminiscent of Petrov-Vodkin), but it is primarily the color itself that is important here. The lighter palette may indicate the influence of Matiushin.

12 N. Adaskina, "Pedagogichesckaia sistema K.S. Petrova-Vodkina," in *Ocherki po russkomu i sovetskomy iskussvtu*, ed. I. Gofman (Lenigrad: Khudozhnik RSFSR, 1974), 286.

13 The number of the figures, their disposition, and the tau cross indicate a non-Russian, perhaps Northern European, compositional source. Ivanova, of course, was familiar with Dutch painting.

14 Petrov-Vodkin also used the blue background in *After the Battle* (1923), *Portrait of Anna Akhmatova* (1924), and several self-portraits (from 1908, 1926-1927, and 1929). The figures are related to other drawings imitative of Petrov-Vodkin's style.

15 Adaskina, "Pedagogicheshkaia sistema," 292.

16 Machmut-Jhashi, "The Art of Kuzma Petrov-Vodkin 1878-1939," 133.

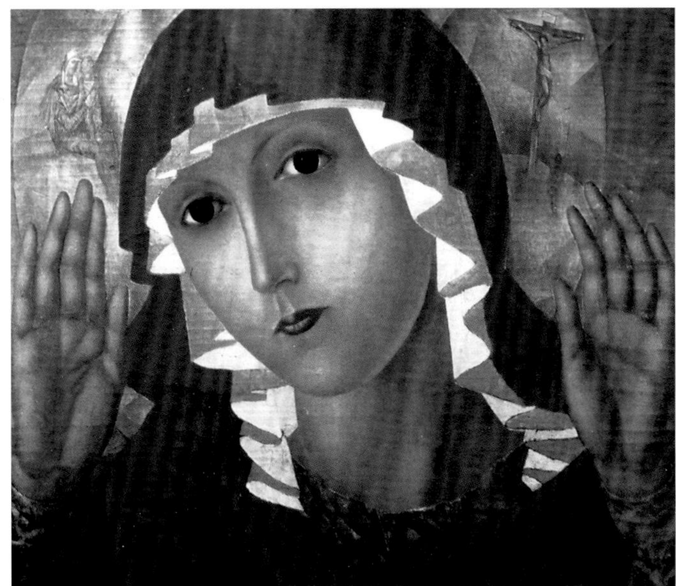

Fig. 30 Kuzma Petrov-Vodkin,
Virgin of Lovingkindness 1920,
oil on canvas, 98 x 109 cm,
Russian Museum

A novel treatment of space [through which] Petrov-Vodkin was able to synthesize the spiritual and formal elements of the perspective system used in icon painting with new notions of space and time resulting from scientific discoveries in physics and mathematics in the early twentieth century. Movement was [a] primary feature of Petrov-Vodkin's spatial theory…He believed that the viewer's movement is tied to the movement of the earth.[17]

Petrov-Vodkin's early painting, *Boys Playing*, is an excellent early example of this handling of space: "The viewer's vantage point was somewhere well above and beyond the surface, a position…that opened up entirely new possibilities of meaning for Petrov-Vodkin's subjects…the sensation conveyed was that a part of the very earth was visible below the figures, and not simply a fragment of ground."[18]

Boys Playing was an important painting for Ivanova; no fewer than five variations survive in her hand. In two versions signed and dated 1922, *Man and Hunched Figure* (B8) and *Two Nudes* (B7), the horizon lines curve and pairs of figures confront each other just as in *Boys Playing*. Multiple viewpoints allow Ivanova to show the top of a female figure's head and arms, the front of her torso, and the side of her legs. Another pair of studies on the same theme, *Linear Study for figural Composition and Study of Two Figures* (D6.2 and D6.3), betray an awareness of the dynamism of Petrov-Vodkin's work in more fluid forms. The abstract sketch has a fully semi-circular "planetary" horizon line anchoring the lines of motion of the two figures. Ivanova's application of Petrov-Vodkin's perspective system is also clear from the watercolor *Kitchen Scene* (fig. 20, C27, p. 43) and the more moderate oil *Still Life with Bread and Butter* (F47). In the common handling of the surfaces, the elevated point of view, and the delicate spatial relations between the objects, Ivanova produces a competent paraphrase of her teacher's technique.[19]

Petrov-Vodkin exercised a formative influence on many aspects of Ivanova's training, an influence evident in her use of color, line, and space. However, he believed "a higher art school should familiarize the student with a wide range of all the accomplishments of contemporary art."[20] Indeed, beyond the pieces that bear the stamp of his personal style, the wealth and variety of Ivanova's work are testimony not only to the environment of remarkable experimentation sanctioned by the fledgling Soviet state in which Ivanova received her artistic education, but also to the validity and integrity of Petrov-Vodkin's influence.

17 Ibid., 123, 131, 133. "World space" combined Renaissance one-point perspective with several non-traditional perspectival systems, including inverse perspective, where lines diverge rather than converge as they recede; spherical perspective (crudely put, a fish-eye effect); and hierarchical perspective, where an object's importance determines its size and appearance, often requiring multiple, moving viewpoints in a single composition.

18 Ibid., 124.

19 The studies *Two Domestic Scenes: One Crossed Out* for the watercolor *Kitchen Scene* indicates that it originally was conceived with figures and with a less dramatic "tilt" that produces the "bird's eye" view of the kitchen interior.

20 Adaskina, "Pedagogicheshkaia sistema," 288.

The Late Landscapes:
Remembering Mikhail Matiushin

ALINA ORLOV

The task of this essay is twofold. First, to offer an appreciation of Ivanova's landscapes in oil from the 1930s and early 1940s—a time when both clarity and serenity graced her hand; second, to consider these landscapes in relation to the work of one of her principal teachers, Mikhail Matiushin (1861-1934),[1] one of last successors to the nineteenth-century Russian landscape tradition and himself a disciple of the experimental landscapist Arkhip Kuindzhi (1841-1910).[2]

Ivanova's late landscapes are unexpected. Nothing in her earlier work—abrasive, anatomical, at times utilitarian, and, for the most part, "avant-garde"—prepares us for her meditative, calm, and interiorized apprehension of nature in the 1930s and 1940s. We can only guess as to what prompted this new sensibility: perhaps she had "matured" or had discovered the pleasure of painting *en plein air* and painting for her own gratification. Then, again, in the prescriptive political climate of the late 1930s, Ivanova may have felt that landscape painting was a secure and innocent genre. But perhaps a deeper reason for Ivanova's rural orientation is to be found in her early artistic education and in her acquaintance with Matiushin and his original ideas about color and space.

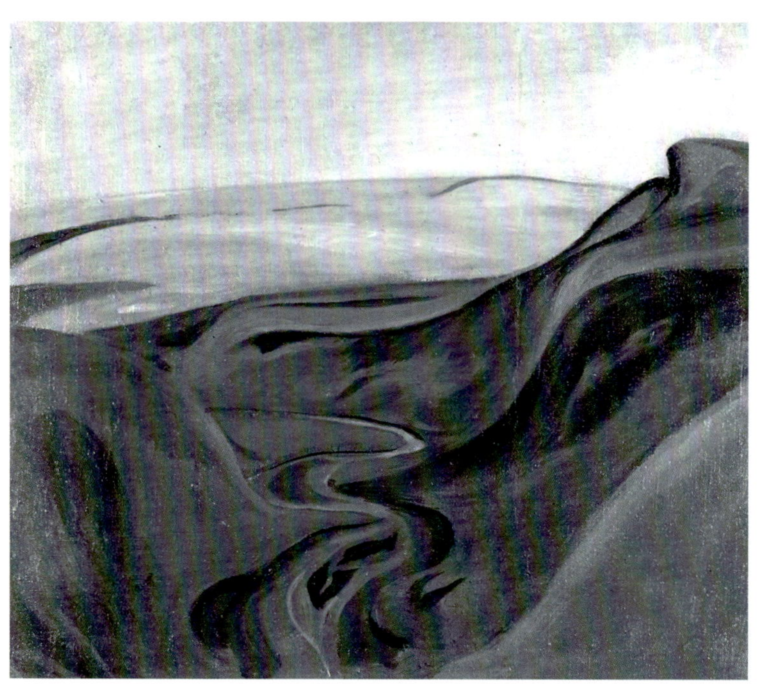

Fig. 31 Mikhail Matuishin, Mountains c. 1908, oil on canvas, Galerie Gmurzynska, Cologne, Germany

As a student at the Academy, Ivanova made copious notes from Matiushin's lectures, even though, curiously enough, her early practical work seems to owe no debt to his teaching. As an aspiring artist, Ivanova was more impressed by other mentors, such as Pavel Filonov and Kuzma Petrov-Vodkin. Her early portraits, for example, suggest formal parallels with Petrov-Vodkin—in the structural make-up of the face and in the predilection for a deep ultramarine blue. Even more obvious in Ivanova's work is the imprint of Filonov's meticulous, organic manner of drawing and composition. Although in the early 1920s, when Ivanova was attending the Academy, Matiushin was a prominent figure and had formed a strong following, Ivanova seems not to have come under his spell. In fact, if it were not for the late landscapes, we might assume that Ivanova had been impervious to Matiushin's remarkable theories of color and space. That Matiushin's ideas returned in Ivanova's landscapes indicates how influence can gestate unseen for a long period of time.

1 The main source of information on Matiushin is Alla Povelikhina, ed., *Matjuschin und die Leningrader Avantgarde*, ex. cat. (Karlsruhe: Zentrum fur Kunst und Medientechnologie, 1991). A second source is *Organica*, ex. cat. (Cologne: Galerie Gmurzynska, 1999).

2 For information on Kuindzhi, see M. Nevedomsky and I. Repin, *Kuindzhi* (St. Petersburg: Kuindzhi Society, 1913); V. Manin, *Kuindzhi i ego shkola* (Leningrad: Khudozhnik RSFSR, 1987).

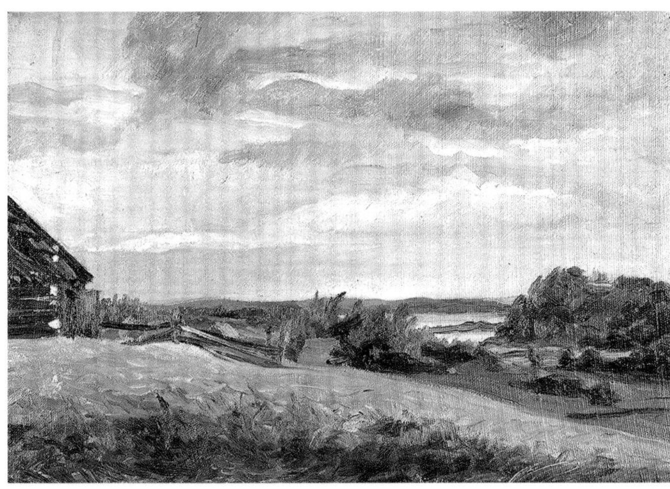

Fig. 32 Edge of House on Green Slope
(F8) 1934-1950

earth. No boundary line stands still and all elements—the land, the trees, the sky—quiver with the impulse to expand. Matiushin's early paintings like *Mountains* (fig. 31), also breathe with the same sense of openness and comprehensive apprehension of space.

Not all of Matiushin's observations of nature are to be found in Ivanova's landscapes. In any case, he was more of a theoretician than was Ivanova and his paintings often function as illustrations of his writings about visual perception and apprehension. The titles of his paintings often bear a direct intellectual relationship to his theories, whereas Ivanova's landscapes are concerned less with theoretical assumptions than with the process itself—which for her was more tactile than analytical. Nevertheless, her late landscapes recall certain elements in Matiushin's approach, including: (a) the depiction of what he called "expanded vision" and the implication of an all-surrounding space; (b) the intensification of color through experimentation with interactions between individual pigments; (c) a specific palette consisting of clean and "unnatural" or quasi-Impressionist colors; (d) an interest in the energy of natural elements (i.e., water, land, and sky) as expressed by the gesture of the human and, therefore, unstable hand.

Matiushin promoted art as an opportunity to expand vision. Explaining his theory of "Zor-Ved" (literally "See-Know"), he bade his students: "Don't teach yourself to memorize, teach yourself to see through the back of your neck, the crown of your head, your temple and even your footprints."[3] In paired works such as *First Landscape in All-around View*[4] and *Second Landscape in All-around View (From Behind)*,[5] the idea was to depict a panoramic view of what lay both in front of and behind the artist, thus capturing a special effect which offers resistance to frames and borders. This resistance can also be seen in Matiushin's painting technique. In *Second Landscape* the brush-strokes defining the land emanate from a "de-centered center" outward to the periphery. The horizon line curves, imitating the earth's spherical form as if this could be perceived by the human eye. The vast sky—the largest part of the composition—contains both movement upwards into infinity and pressure downwards on the trees that compliment the edge of the

Although Ivanova's artistic worlds are not filled with such a dramatic sense of spatial expansion, she evinces a similar interest in destabilizing the boundary line—a concern manifest in her approach to the very materiality of her paintings, especially her use of the irregularly cropped piece of cloth. She seemed not to have cared that the edges of her canvases were uneven and ragged and did not constitute perfect quadrangles. She rarely stretched the cloth onto a frame and she refused even to cut the borderline cross and at a right angle. This refusal reflects Ivanova's own æsthetic of boundaries. In a sense, the first mark Ivanova made with her brush on a clean canvas was already her fifth, since the edges already functioned as lines with which the first brush stroke engaged itself. The first four lines in Ivanova's landscapes can thus be regarded as the initial or original ones shaping the canvas. The logic behind the decision to either cut or accept a crooked framework is to reject fixed and correct boundaries—a logic more appropriate to natural space than to a neat and tidy edge. In other words, Ivanova's concession to the "ragged" format implies that it is more appropriate to see natural space within an imperfect or organic rectangle.

Let us look at *Edge of House on Green Slope* (fig. 32, F8) as an exercise in Ivanova's rendering of natural space. Although her primary intention seems not to present a higher, mystical experience of spaciousness (as was often the case with Matiushin), Ivanova nonetheless achieves this in *Edge of House on Green Slope*, albeit in subtle ways reinforced by the careless cut of the frame. Here, the unruly borders call more attention to themselves than in other paintings and the bottom edge is cut so unevenly that it disturbs the visual world within the frame, thus rejecting the apparent comfort that conventional borders bring. The four circles at the corners reveal, traces of the pins and revealing the gesso underpainting, serve also to stave off the artifice of illusion, just as Ivanova's borders try to work against artificiality. This kind of self-reflective commentary points to the artistic process itself and

3 M. Matiushin, "Ne iskusstvo, a zhizn," *Zhizn iskusstva* 20 (Petrograd, 1923): 15.
4 Matiushin, *First Landscape in All-Around View*, 1924, watercolor on paper, 22.2 x 34.3 cm, RM.
5 Matiushin, *Second Landscape in All-Around View (from Behind)*, 1924, watercolor on paper, 22.3 x 27.9 cm, RM.

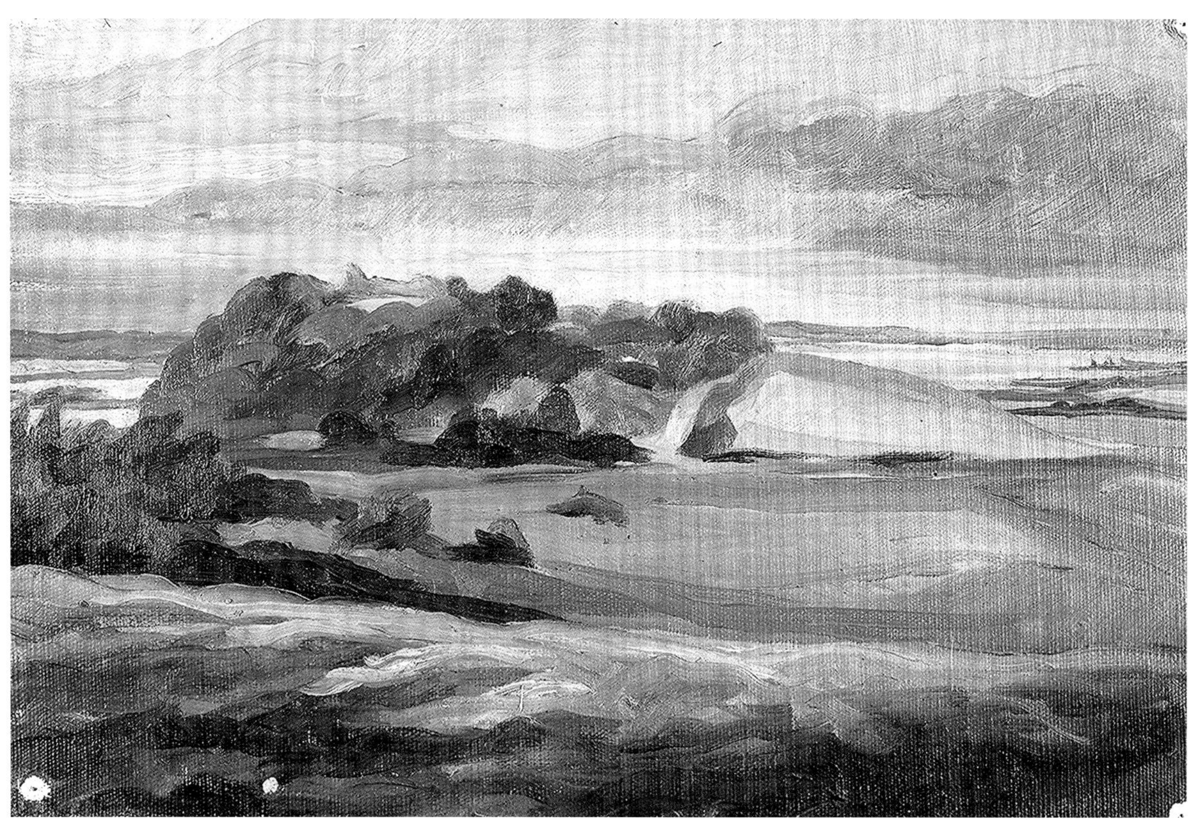

Fig. 34 Landscape with Hill in Midground
(F9) late 1930s

reveals the falsity of traditional artistic conventions: Ivanova is maintaining her commitment to the avant-garde.

Moreover, in the painting process itself, Ivanova disregarded the fixity of borders in *Edge of House on Green Slope* and in other horizontally-oriented landscapes, where the brush strokes move left-to-right and right-to-left across the middle, through the sky and grass, as if transporting the viewer outside the frame. If we try to reconstruct the sequence, we can imagine that, having pinned the cloth to a board, Ivanova painted beyond the canvas edge, onto the board itself. Indeed, if we look closely at the edges of the canvas in *Edge of House on Green Slope* and *Landscape with Hill in Midground* (fig. 34, F9), for example, we find that the paint has accumulated thickly where the brush scraped across the left and right edges. In some places, the cloth is even slightly saturated with pigment on the reverse side. Working with a canvas loosely

stretched directly on a board seems to have facilitated this process of coloring outside the line. As a result, the horizontal gestures in these works invite us to move freely across and beyond the canvas.

Indeed, Ivanova's landscapes hearken back not only to Matiushin's conception of space, but also to that of color. Matiushin supervised a laboratory whose investigations in color perception formed the basis of his celebrated treatise, *The Laws of Change in Color Combinations* (1932).[6] Furthermore, this research left an immediate imprint on his own palette, one that was unique among his contemporaries in its privileging of clean, bright, colors intensely filled with light, and separated from one another as with the off-greens, light pinks, blues, and mauves of his landscapes. Matiushin also used watercolor in such a way that he maintained the integrity of the individual pigment. He wrote in 1926-1927: "Sound has the same oscillation as color. And the words 'a crimson tone,' a thin,

6 M. Matiushin, *Spravochnik po tsvetu. Zakonomernost izmeniaemosti tsvetovykh sochetanii* (Leningrad: OGIZ, 1932).

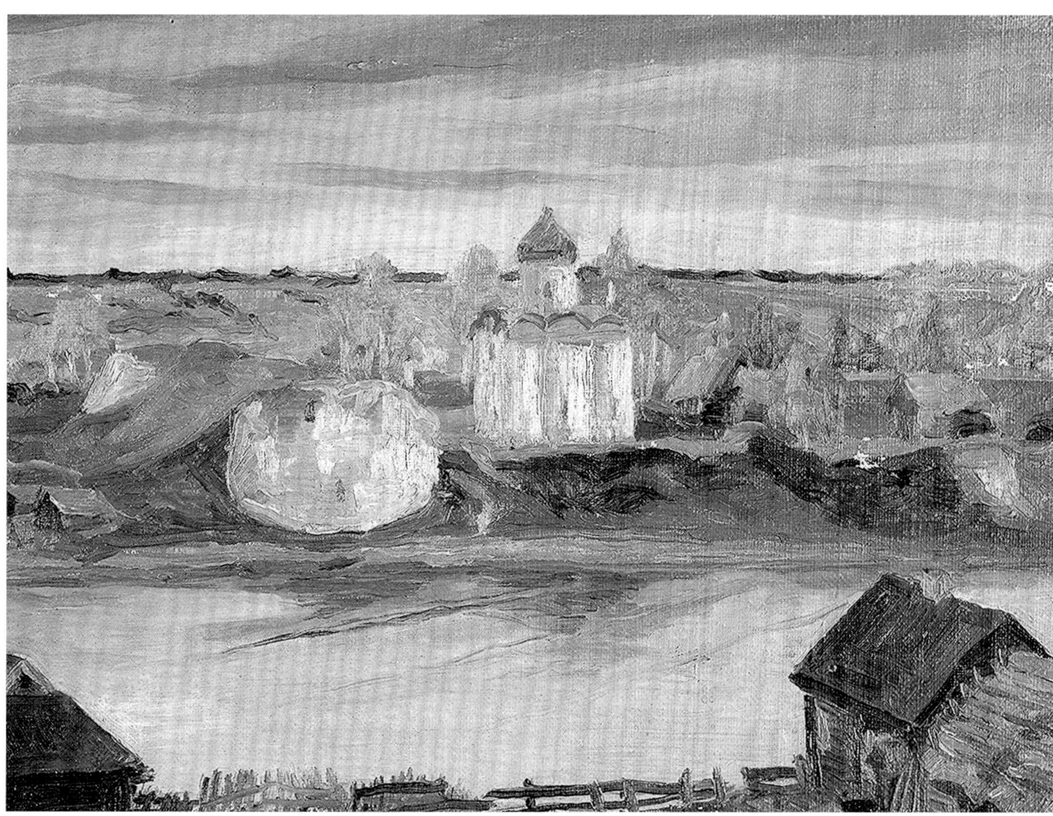

Fig. 35 Church and Other Buildings on the Bank of a River (F7) 1934-1950

thick, transparent, brilliant or dull sound determine and show very clearly that our eye, as it were, can hear and our ear can see."[7]

Although Ivanova's palette appears muted and muddied and her use of color more visceral than studied, some of her landscapes bear a striking similarity to Matiushin's in terms of their color conception. The intensity of the green in *River in Hilly Landscape* (F3), while recalling the curved horizon and distanced huts of Matiushin's *First Landscape*, also evokes the saturated purity of pigments, an impression Matiushin worked endlessly to create. Moreover, both Matiushin's and Ivanova's landscapes rely on Impressionist color devices where myriad different colors exist in remarkably close proximity, interplaying, and yet retaining their integrity. The forest in Matiushin's *First Landscape*, for example, shows a variety of coexisting pigments of blue, green, brown, black, and orange. Similarly, any square section across the middle horizon of another of Ivanova's landscapes, *Single Tree with Purple Flowers* (F2), contains numerous colors—blues, browns, yellows— some of which are not repeated twice.

Ivanova's relationship to color may have been sensuous and intuitive, but she also took account of certain principles of color-perception. The works *Church and Other Buildings on the Bank of a River* (F7) and *Summer Landscape with Sunflowers* (F37) are characteristic of her way of assigning light and muted blues and violet hues to the background, while reserving the bright greens and yellows for spaces that needed to come forward. Each color towards the front also has a higher degree of separation or contrast in relation to the next, resulting in curious ambiguities and perceptions of depth.

7 M. Matiushin, "Nauka v ickusstve," 1926-1927, unpublished manuscript, Institute of Russian Liteature, St. Petersberg, as quoted in, A. Povelikhina, "Matyushin" Spatial System," *The Structurists* 15-16 (1975): 69.

In Search of the Self: Ivanova and the Primitive

RIKA IEZUMI

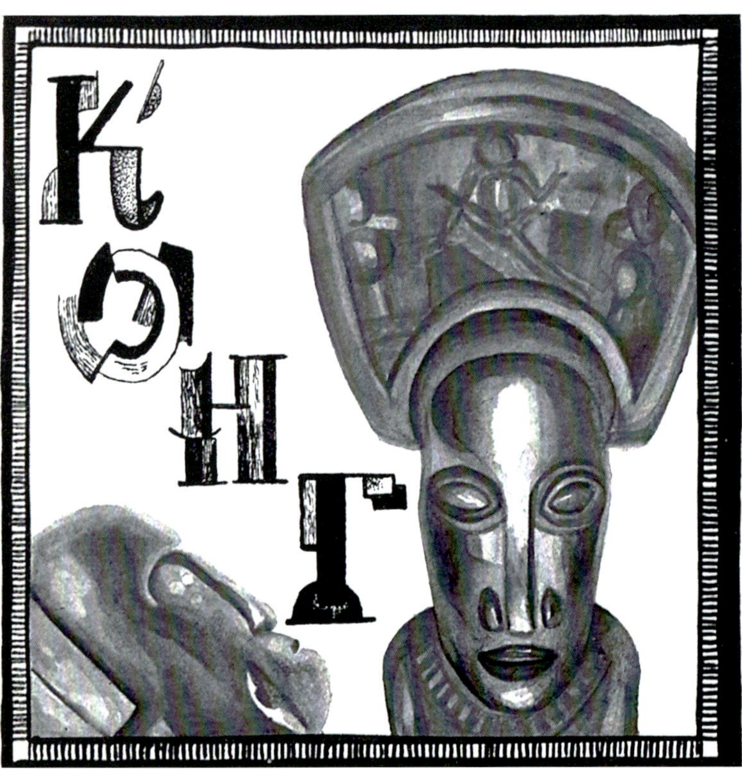

Fig. 36 Design for Congo Cigarette Packaging
(E2) January 18, 1926

"PRIMITIVE ART FORMS—ICONS, LUBKI, TRAYS, SIGNBOARDS, FABRICS OF THE EAST, ETC.—THESE ARE SPECIMENS OF GENUINE VALUE AND PAINTERLY BEAUTY." Alexander Shevchenko[1]

In 1913, the artist and theorist Alexander Shevchenko published a manifesto entitled Neo-Primitivism, in which he commented on the current Russian and European fascination with what he called "primitive" sources such as peasant art, children's art, and the art of the East. Although of a later generation, Liudmila Ivanova was also drawn to this subject and a number of her paintings and drawings of the 1920s carry "primitive" images of Egypt, Africa, and China. Inasmuch as Ivanova created these works while a student at the Academy of Arts in Leningrad, the immediate influence of her teachers and their pedagogical curricula should be regarded as a major stimulus to her interest in primitivism. The main purpose of this essay is to examine this particular fragment of Ivanova's legacy and to position it within the general scope of her varied and multifaceted *œuvre*.

To discuss the pictorial elements of Africa, China, and similar "alternative" cultures—in other words, the "primitive" and the "other" as refracted in nineteenth and twentieth century European art—is to invite a response of suspicion and mistrust.[2] Certainly, a Chinese head or an Egyptian ornament in Ivanova's works may be read as images of the "other," but this provisional category does not necessarily imply geographical distinction or an inseperable division between West and East. According to Susan Miller, the category of the "other" may also include the "inhabitants of the realms of supernatural beings and monsters and is used to define a self or a society."[3] Nonetheless, for the West, the non-West has tended (and continues) to evoke the notion of the "primitive" and non-contemporary, which may explain the parallel usage of the term "other," especially in debates concerning the modern period. Picasso's incorporation of Black African sculpture into his studio art exemplifies the apparent connections between the "primitive," "Primitivism," and the "other." According to Robert Goldwater, one of the first art historians to explore the dialogue between Primitivism and modern

1 Alexander Shevchenko, "Neo-primitivism," (1913) ed. and trans. John E. Bowlt, in *Russian Art of the Avant-Garde: Theory and Criticism 1902-1934* (London: Thames and Hudson, 1988), 45.

2 Ivanova's art of "primitivist" images should also be seen in the context of Filonov's injunction to his students: "Students must work on still-lifes, ethnograhical and revolutionaries from photographs. They should also work on abstract paintings, political pictures, political satires, caricatures and anti-religious subjects, lubki, covers, posters, toys, handicraft items, sculpture, woodcarving, wallpaper, designs for plates, cups, carpets, trays and balaikas, and they should also make signboards and ads using all kind of lettering." Pavel Filonov to Yan Lukstyn, 1928, reproduced in *Pavel Filonov: A Hero and His Fate*, Nicoletta Misler and John E. Bowlt (Austin, TX: Silvergirl, 1983), 287.

3 Susan Miller, ed., *The Myth of Primitivism: Perspectives on Art* (London, New York: Routledge, 1991), 11.

art, the individual artist (in this case, Picasso) sees himself as superior and proceeds to create a "primitive" object by revisiting a "primitive style" derived from African artifacts while ignoring the cultural context of the object. On this level, then, "primitive" objects serve merely as a source of æsthetic inspiration for the Western artist.[4]

But this formal commitment is not the only aspect in the issue of Primitivism and modern art. Gill Perry argues, for example, that primitive art was inflected with the notions of the "decorative," the "expressive," and the "authentic," and that "each [artist] had different approaches to the images of the 'other' or the 'primitive' as in the cases of the French Symbolists and the German Expressionists." Furthermore, Perry emphasizes that for many modern artists the significant and fundamental aspect of "Primitivism" was the use of the "primitive" to critique of particular artistic values and conventions."[5]

The numerous references to the "primitive" and the "Oriental" in early twentieth century Russian art (such as a turbaned man or a pyramid gracing a pack of cigarettes) reflected a pronounced fashion in international design of the time: "Basic geometry and boldly clarified color could be yoked with eye-catching typographic elements and a telegraphic style of diction, to disrupt the numbering routines of tradition, and to open convergent routes toward the irresistible communication of the government's credo."[6] In Russia, however, the basic concept of "primitivism" would seem to be rather different. As Shevchenko announced, "we are called barbarians, Asians"[7] and certain artists of the avant-garde (above all, Natalia Goncharova and Mikhail Larionov) even equated Russia with the East and, hence, the "primitive."[8] In short, the Russian Neo-Primitivists regarded primitive art as a genesis, adding the prefix "neo" so as to denote an "updating" or adjustment. Ivanova's mentors also seem to have embraced this view of the "primitive"—for

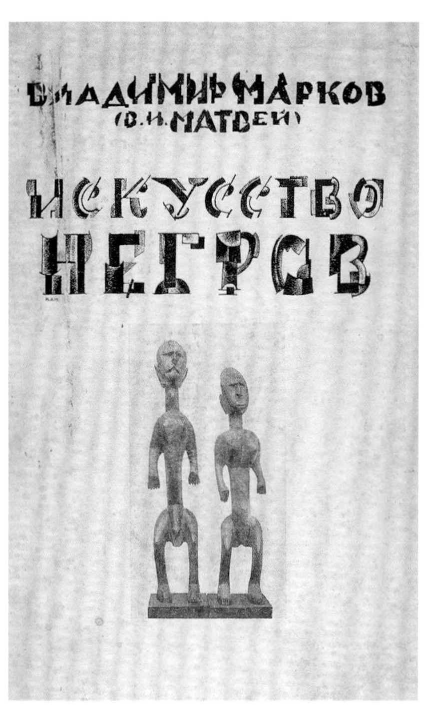

Fig. 37
The Art of Negroes,
by Vlasimir Markov,
1919.
Cover design
by Natan Altman.
These two sculptures
from Nigeria exhibited
at Musée d'
Ethnogrophie du
Trocadero
(now Musée de
l'Homme) Paris.

instance, Petrov-Vodkin's through his interest in the Mediaeval icon, Mikhail Matiushin's through his eclectic study of peasant toys and Buddhism, and Pavel Filonov's through his appeal to Russian folk art on the one hand and to Persian philosophy on the other.

Ivanova seems to have applied such imagery of the "primitive" and the "other" almost indiscriminately, both decoratively (in her 1926 designs for cigarette packages) and in works of political and anti-religious propaganda, as in *Between China and France* (C21) and *Christ is Risen* (fig. 40, C22, p. 59). She juxtaposes sphinxes, pyramids, lions, and mummies against fantastic cityscapes in such works as *Serpents and Idols* (C18), *Design with Egyptian Motifs* (C19), *Crucifixion with Pioneer Boy* (fig. 41, C23, p. 59), *Sphinx with Central Asian Head* (C30), and *A Woman Smoking a Pipe* (C32); or

4   Inspired very much by Robert Goldwater, William Rubin organized the controversial exhibition "Primitivism in 20th Century Art: Affinity of the Tribal and the Modern" at the Museum of Modern Art, New York, in 1984. Rubin attempted to establish formal affinities between modern artists and "primitive" art/artifacts by the strategic juxtaposition of key artifacts.

5   Gill Perry, "Primitivism and the 'Modern,'" *Primitivism, Cubism, Abstraction: the Early Twentieth Century* (New Haven, London: Yale University Press, 1993), 35-74, 82.

6   Kirk Varnedoe and Adam Gopnik eds., *High and Low: Modern Art and Popular Culture*, ex. cat. (New York: Abrams, 1991), 55.

7   Shevchenko, 49.

8   Mikhail Larionov and Natalia Goncharova, "Rayonists and Futurists: A Manifesto," trans. John E. Bowlt, *Russian Art of the Avant-Garde*, 90. Larinov and Goncharova declare: "Long live the beautiful East! We are joining forces with contemporary Eastern artists to work together. Long live nationality! We march hand in hand with our ordinary house painters. Long live the style of rayonist painting that we created—free from concrete forms, existing and developing according to painterly laws."

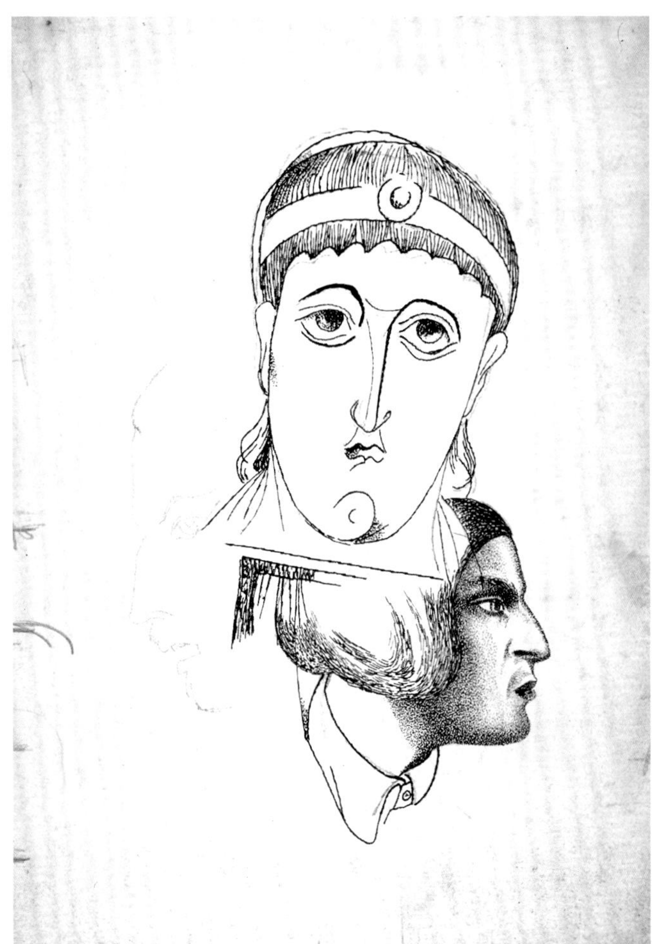

Egyptian head, two Greek heads, African sculptures) and her choice
of style (geometric shapes, bold letters for the name of the product)
connect immediately with similar practices in Western Europe
and the United States. The design for *Congo Cigarettes* (fig. 36, E2)
is a case in point: the composition incorporates two African sculptures—one frontal and occupying the right half of the composition,
the other in diagonal profile in the lower left corner—modeled on
Congolese sculptures illustrated in artist and theorist Vladimir
Markov's study Iskusstvo negrov [*The Art of Negroes*] (published
posthumously in 1919); furthermore, the decorative letters "KONG"
are in the exact same style as Natan Altman's title for the cover
of Markov's book.[9] Ivanova's obvious familiarity with and debt to
Markov's book allows us to assess his analyses of the "other" as
they relate to this discussion. Markov (the pseudonym of
Waldemars Matvejs, 1877-1914) was a member of the Union of
Youth, a group of radical artists active in pre-Revolutionary St.
Petersburg,[10] and a close associate of Ivanova's mentors, Filonov
and Matiushin. Markov, an outstanding theorist who promoted
Oriental (what he termed "primitive") art, was the first Russian
scholar to examine African, Chinese, and Polynesian art forms as
æsthetic artifacts rather than as anthropological documents.

she focuses on Chinese motifs like the Chinese head, Buddha, and
the word "Shanghai" in *Christ is Risen*, and on wild and exotic animals as in *Head with Generic Native Imagery: Koala and Alligator*
(C40, C41). Commercial advertisements like the cigarette packs
provided Ivanova with an especially rich field of "primitive" application: some are simple line drawings with a single image; others are
more abstract, intricate compositions; some are monochrome in ink
or pencil or both, while others are painted. True, there are several
elements in Ivanova's œuvre that cannot be accommodated easily
within these rudimentary categories such as the bizarre beasts or
Byzantine heads and a full discussion of the "primitive" in Ivanova's
entire oeuvre lies beyond the parimeters of this essay.

The applied designs of the 1920s are instructive as a microcosmic
display of Ivanova's interpretation of the "primitive" because her
choice of the "primitive" references (e.g., the profile of a sphinx, an

Judging from his essays, "The Principles of the New Art" and "The
Principle of Free Creation," what impelled Markov to study "primitive" art was the "intuition" and "fortuitousness" of Oriental,
Byzantine, and Greek art, which he contrasted with the logic and
science of Western Europe.[11] A significant component of Markov's
theoretical appreciation of Black African art was what he called
the "non-constructiveness" of "primitive" art; Markov hoped that
through this "non-constructiveness," in other words, irrational and
unscientific basis, Russian art would attain a spiritual liberation.
In this respect, Markov was close to the German Expressionists'
and Vasilii Kandinsky's rejection of academic convention and their
discovery of a new emotional freedom.

So, was Ivanova a Primitivist? As far as Congo Cigarettes is concerned it would hardly seem to be non-constructive; however,

9 See plates 112 and 113 of Vladimir Markov's *Iskusstvo negrov* (Petrograd: NKP, 1919), 143. This book is primarily
about African sculptures and masks in various ethnographical collections, especially in Dusseldorf and Leiden.
Markov's essay on African art is accompanied by a preface written by his companion, Varvara Bubnova. See
Takizawa Kyoji and Harata Atsuko, *Bubnova* 1886-1983 (Tokyo: Committee of the Varvara Bubnova Exhibition, 1995), 20.
10 For information on the Union of Youth see Jeremy Howard, *The Union of Youth: An Artists' Society of the Russian
Avant-Garde* (New York: St. Martin's Press, 1992).
11 Vladimir Markov, "the Principles of the New Art," "Principles of Free Creation." In *Russian Art of the Avant–Guarde*,
ed. and trans. John E. Bowlt (London: Thames and Hudson, 1988)

Ivanova's approach connects with Perry's definition of "primitivism," in its emphasis on the purely decorative element and its freedom from convention.[12] Although Ivanova shared this emphasis with the French Symbolists, she is less concerned with the transmission of lofty ideas and intense emotions through color and form; rather, she uses African imagery simply as a marketing device. Yet, was Ivanova eager to free herself from artistic convention? So it seems. For example, in *Christ is Risen*, Ivanova included Chinese and Christian motifs alongside a comical Buddha, a Chinese (more precisely, a Manchurian) head, temple-like architecture, a serpent, a fig, and a cross. Here is neither praise nor censure, although perhaps the ridiculously small and chubby Buddha refers to—and criticizes—Matiushin's sympathy for the Buddhist worldview. Similarly, the staked Chinese head in the *Two Heads: Frontal Byzantine and Modern Profile* (fig. 38, C15) should perhaps be read as a rejection of Filonov's influence. Here, a simple, stylized Byzantine head (Markov regarded Byzantine art as "primitive"), painted in a forceful style of controlled abrupt contours, overlays a woman in profile whose head is rendered with short staccato lines—the essence of Filonov's concept of "madeness." Perhaps, then, Ivanova's varied approaches to painting, drawing, and design at this time, especially her complex accumulation of "primitive" and "other" references, can be accepted as manifestations of a search for stylistic and psychological independence.

In the late 1920s and early 1930s Ivanova's passion for experimental art seems to have waned, perhaps because she discovered a new vocation as a museum curator and literary editor. However, in her diary entry for 12 September 1934, she utters a *cri de coeur*: "I was painting and my tears were rushing down over my face, my hands, the easel…for the first time in these years I was sorry that I had quit painting… And I was painting from the sketch that I had made from inside the canyon, a view of Cherkes-Kerman in the mountains… I drew everything with the brush only. All the colors are delineated, all the shapes are clean cut. Light and shadow. Everything is in place."[13] Here was an artistic rebirth, one inspired by the archaeological expedition to northern Russia that her second husband, Vladislav Ravdonikas, undertook in 1934. Ivanova seems to have created several interpretations of that wild region, using them, among other things, as illustrations and designs for Ravdonikas's two volume work *Naskalnye izobrazheniia Onezhskogo ozera i Belogo moria* [Cliff Drawings of Onezh Lake and the White Sea] (1936 and 1938).[14] Thus, exposure to the "primitive" in the form of the ancient civilizations of northern Russia rekindled Ivanova's passion for painting—not Filonov or Matiushin. No doubt, at this point Ivanova could have echoed Markov's words at the discovery of the "primitive" and the pristine strength of childhood:

> Where concrete reality, the tangible, ends, there begins another world—a world of unfathomed mystery, a world of the Divine. Even primitive man was given the chance of approaching this boundary, where intuitively he would capture some feature of the Divine—and return happy as a child. And he sought to introduce it into the confines of the tangible and to secure it there while finding forms to express it; at the same time he attempted to find ways by which he would be able to encounter and sense once again an analogous beauty.[15]

Thereafter, Ivanova produced numerous landscape paintings, treading the "path of the ancient prototype of the *Kalevala*."[16] In Markov's system, Ivanova's depictions of the Russian landscape and the simple Russian church from the late 1930s might be evocations of the "primitive" or the "other," although they might also be construed as mute protests against the false rhetoric of Socialist Realism.

12 Perry, Primitivism and the 'Modern,' 82.
13 See Felix Ravdonikas, "My Mother, Liudmila Ivanova" in this catalog.
14 Vladislav Ravdonikas, *Nasakalnye izobrazheniia Onezhskogo ozera i Belogo moria* (Moscow, Leningrad: Academy of Arts of USSR, Vol. 1, 1936; Vol. 2, 1938).
15 Markov, "The Principles of the New Art," 25.
16 See Ravdonikas, in this catalog.

Seeing Is Not Believing: Ivanova and Religion

WALTER MEYER

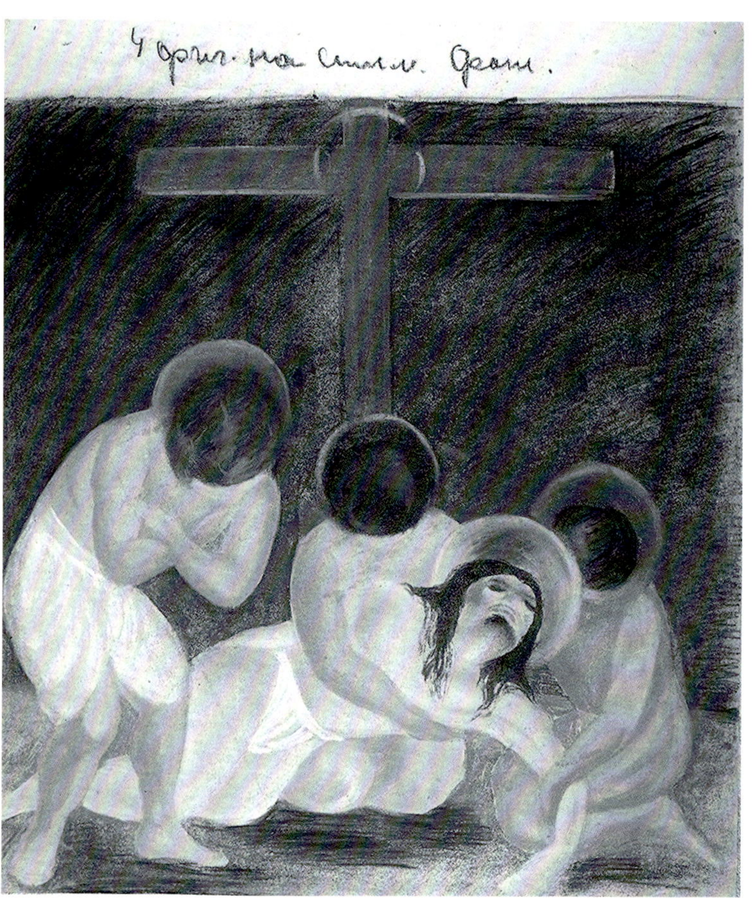

Fig. 39 Four Figures on a Blue Background (B13) c. 1923

After Vladimir Iliich Lenin's ascension to power as head of the new Bolshevik state in Russia in 1917, Karl Marx's declaration of religion as the "opium of the masses"[1] assumed a harsh, even militant tone. "Every religious idea, every idea of God, even flirting with the idea of God, is unutterable vileness,"[2] Lenin declared. The Bolshevik regime sought to suppress religious practices and ideas, replacing, for example, religious instruction in schools with the science of atheism. Particular attention was paid to breaking the hold of the Orthodox Church, which, on 23 January 1918, was stripped of the right to own property and, consequently, of its financial base. On the eve of the Revolution, there were over 50,000 active churches in the Russian Empire; by the late 1930s, only a few hundred remained. Many had been destroyed, others were converted into commercial centers or warehouses. Notwithstanding these draconian measures, some scholars believe that after an initial decline the 1920s witnessed an upsurge in religious awareness.[3]

From the outset of the Bolshevik regime, artists were involved in the campaign against religion and, presumably, Ivanova created her anti-religious pieces as assignments within the new and radical Academy of Arts. Several of these images are unfinished, but it is difficult to understand how they could have functioned as practical instruments of anti-religious propaganda. As exercises within the Academy, Ivanova's visual responses to the theme of religion are, therefore, more than mere extensions of Party jargon and indicate the complexity of individual responses to the break with traditional religious practices and attitudes toward religion.

Four Figures on a Blue Background (fig. 39, B13), one of Ivanova's early works, is an example of the confused or, at least, ambiguous attitudes toward religion that characterized the 1920s.[4] In this scene of Christ's deposition, three haloed figures, their faces positioned to obscure their features, surround Christ's limp body as it is taken from the cross. Although there is little to indicate animosity toward religion, the inscription "4 figures on a blue background" across the top subverts any iconographical empathy with the subject-matter by laying stress not on the sacred story or symbols of Christian piety, but on the compositional and formal elements: the scene is merely four figures on a blue background. Indeed, Ivanova

1 Jon Elster, ed., *Karl Marx: A Reader* (Cambridge: Cambridge University Press, 1986), 301.

2 V. I. Lenin, *Sochineniia* (Moscow: Gosizdat, 1952) vol. 35: 89-90.

3 Philip Walters, "A Survey of Soviet Religious Policy," in *Religious Policy in the Soviet Union*, ed. Sabrina Petra Ramet (New York: Cambridge University Press, 1993), 5-7. Another useful source for understanding the Bolshevik battle against religion is René Fulop Miller, *Mind and Face of Bolshevism* (London: Putnam, 1927).

4 Stylistically, this work resembles other works known to be from Ivanova's early years at the Academy and can, therefore, be dated to 1923.

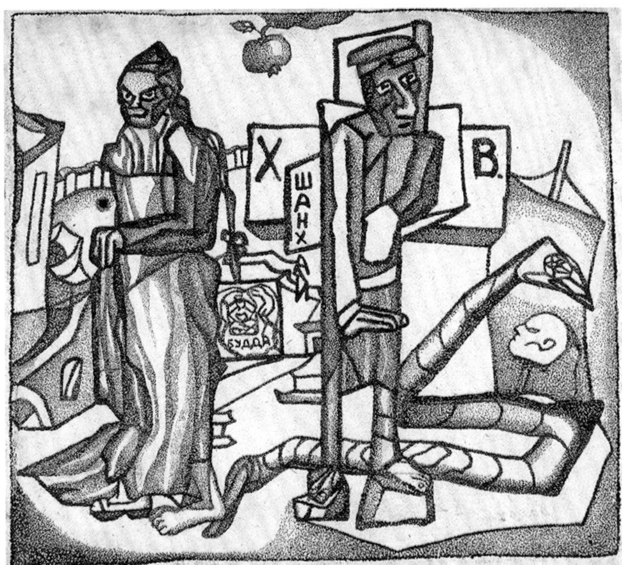

Fig. 40 Christ is Risen (C22) 1925

an anti-religious commentary? The pessimistic mood of the image begs the viewer to question what religion has provided: Christ is risen, yet the lot of humanity has not improved. Indeed, perhaps the central figure is not Christ at all, since the absence of a halo and his common clothes hardly signify a Lord and Savior; rather, the image may be of a working man crucified by or for his religious beliefs. True, if this picture had been intended as a cartoon or poster, the attendant caption would have made its meaning less opaque.

created this work while studying under Mikhail Matiushin, a connection that permits us to view the work as a drawing illustrative of his color theory; the halos may even be extensions of Matiushin's system of circular and expanded vision, a concept that Ivanova applies elsewhere (e.g., her *Untitled Portrait,* fig. 19, p. 42).[5] This rendering of the deposition is not unlike the conversion of churches to utilitarian spaces, i.e., the religious image is reduced to a compositional and æsthetic device. In treating the image of the deposition as being merely a formal exercise, Ivanova may have sought to deprive that image of its power to transmit other, more spiritualized meanings; however, we should also remember that in an atmosphere hostile to religion, one of the few ways to depict religious imagery was in the form of anti-religion. In other words, the image could be manipulated to serve both Bolshevik ideology and private meditation.

Christ is Risen (fig. 40, C22), one of Ivanova's first explicitly anti-religious works, depicts a proletarian Christ standing alone. Behind Christ, there is a cross flanked by the Cyrillic letters "X" and "B" (signifying "Christ is Risen"), while the name "Shanghai" (a primary destination of the White emigration after the Civil War), is written along the left side of the cross. Just below and to the left are a pagoda motif and a small figure within a square labeled "Buddha," direct references to Eastern religious practices. On the right, directly under the serpent's head is a Manchurian figure whose head is impaled upon a stick.[6] The female figure in the foreground may refer to Mary (her heel steps on the serpent's tail, a Christian reading of Genesis 3:15), who holds a bitten apple. The pomegranate at the top may reflect Christian symbolism of the multiplication of God's people. While the individual fragments of this image are accessible, their combined meaning is not—so how would they function as

This kind of apparent ambiguity or inconsistency within the image is quintessential to the system of Pavel Filonov, Ivanova's primary artistic mentor in the late 1920s. In both his pre-and post-Revolutionary works, Filonov often drew upon Christian iconography. The celebrated *Feast of the Kings* (oil and watercolor versions, 1912 and 1913, RM) is reminiscent of some bizarre Last Supper, while many of his works contain the images of fish and loaves of bread. Filonov was a devout Orthodox Christian before the Revolution, even making a pilgrimage to Jerusalem and painting icons; after the Revolution, he embraced atheism and Communism, while maintaining his ascetic lifestyle. As in life, so in art, the Filonovian style is subversive inasmuch as it identifies individual signs but not meanings in the overall composition.

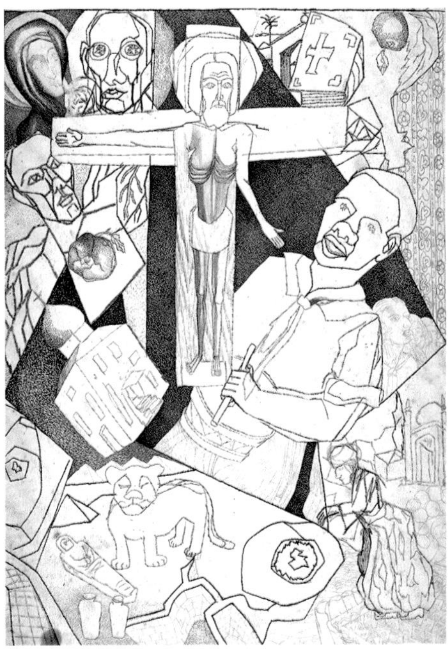

Fig. 41
Crucifixion with Pioneer Boy
(C23) 1925-1927

5 On Ivanova and Mikhai Matiushin, see Alina Orlov, "The Late Landscapes: Remembering Mikhail Matiushin" in this catalog.

6 On Ivanova and the "primitive," see Rika Iezumi, "In Search of the Self: Ivanova and the Primitive" in this catalog.

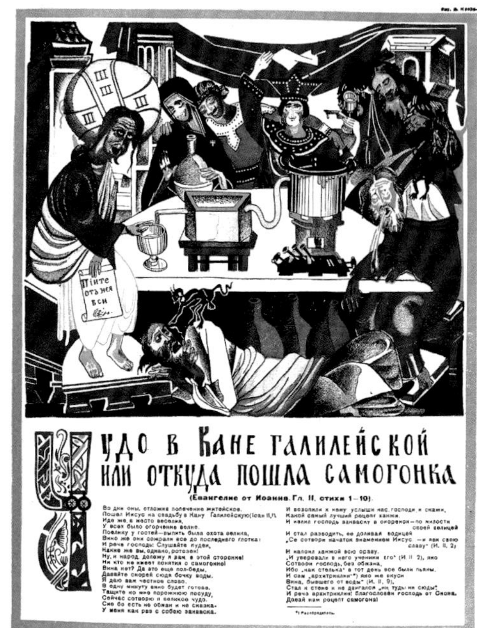

ЧУДО В КАНЕ ГАЛИЛЕЙСКОЙ
ИЛИ ОТКУДА ПОШЛА САМОГОНКА
(Евангелие от Иоанна. Гл. II. стихи 1—10).

Во дни оны, отложив попечение житейское,
Пошел Иисус на свадьбу в Кану Галилейскую (Иоан II,1)
Иде же, в место веселия,
У всех было огорчение волие,
Поелику у гостей—выпить была охота велика,
Вино же они сожрали все до последнего глотка!
И рече господь: Слушайте, люди,
Наже же вы, однако, ротозеи!
Ну, и народ, доложу я вам, в этой сторонке!
Ни кто не имеет понятия о самогонке!
Вина нет? Да это еще пол-беды,
Давайте скорей сюда бочку воды.
Я даю вам честное слово,
В одну минуту вино будет готово,
Тащите ко мне порожнюю посуду,
Сейчас сотворю я великое чудо.
Сие бо есть не обман и не сказка,
У меня как раз с собою закваска.

И возопили к нему услыши нас, господи, и скажи,
Какой самый лучший рецепт ханжи,
И налил господь закваску в огореон—по милости
своей великой
И стал разводить, ее доливая водкой
„Се сотвори начаток знамением Иисус.—и яви свою
славу" (И. II, 2;
И напоил ханжой всю ораву.
„И уверовали в него ученики его" (И II 2), яко
Сотвори господь, без обмана,
Ибо „как стелька" в тот день все были пьяны,
И сам „архитриклин"*) яко же вкуси
Вина, бывшего от воды" (И. II, 9),
Стал к стене и не двигался „ни туды ни сюды",
И рече архитриклин: благословен господь от Сиона,
Давай нам рецепт самогона!

*) Распорядитель

Fig. 42 Anonymous, *Marriage At Cana*
page from "BEZBOZHNIK", 1920s

Ivanova's *Crucifixion with Pioneer Boy* (fig. 41, C23) maintains this complexity of signs.[7] A Pioneer boy ignores the haloed Christ on the cross gesturing towards him; oblivious, the Pioneer beats a drum as he advances amid images of various religions. On the left is a traditional Russian Church, its cross still intact;[8] a pomegranate and two unidentifiable figures with the Virgin Mary fill the upper left corner; Christ occupies the center of the composition, a Bible to the right of his head; in the lower right and left corners, respectively, are a Mosque with a stylized worshipper and the Egyptian imagery of a cat along with a mummy and pyramid.

This eclectic assortment of images may be compared to the museums of religion and atheism instituted at this time to expose the alleged corruption of the church and to discredit religion as a philosophical system incompatible with rational, scientific progress.[9] The largest of these museums, housed in the converted St. Isaac and Kazan Cathedrals in the heart of Leningrad, contained scientific data and "supernatural" objects innocuously displayed inside museum cases.[10] Ivanova's distribution of images around the Pioneer scout functions in much the same way as the juxtaposition of objects in these museums; the inclusion of the Egyptian artifacts along with Christian and Muslim signs elicits uniform equivocation. Just as the science of archaeology was exposing and documenting Egyptian culture and religious practices (which must have seemed absurd to the common Russian), the grouping of such imagery alongside the more common Christian images implies that Christianity is just another irrational tenet. This is not, however, the only potential meaning of the work, for the Christ figure is strangely animated and powerful. Centrally positioned in the front so that nothing but the Pioneer's hand overlaps the cross, Christ is set off from the rest of the composition and engages the viewer. What are we to make of this Christ, strangely sure of himself and neither pathetic nor marginalized? Both before and after the Revolution, reinterpretations of Christ proliferated, including that of theomachy and god-building, which some then identified as the unlimited potential of the new Soviet Man. In this paradigm, the pilgrim is told that he can be like God and that, through Communism, he will join the ranks of the eternal. Christ, then, is demystified and placed within the context of building the new Soviet State, the true paradise. *Together We Will Climb Up to Heaven and Chase Out All the Gods* (fig. 11, C37, p. 32) also treats of the Orthodox Church. As in the other pictures, Ivanova includes a variety of religious themes without investing them with a cohesive meaning. In the center, Mary on the cross holds Jesus as the angel Gabriel flies in with a Lily (symbol of the Annunciation). These symbols provide the context within which Ivanova censures the abuses of the Orthodox Church: Mary and Gabriel seem to be emerging from a jar of moonshine placed in front of Grigorii Rasputin; Rasputin, celebrated for his hypnotic powers and identified here by his large, enticing eyes and peasant shirt of good cloth, holds a fistful of radiant, gem-like rubles. To the right of Gabriel is a priest, most likely Pitrim, the Metropolitan of Petrograd, who attained his position of power with the help of Rasputin. In his left hand, the Metropolitan wields an incense holder shaped like a morning star, while his right reaches for a bottle of

<hr>

7 Both *Crucifixion with Pioneer Boy* and *Together We Will Climb Up to Heaven* are undated but can be placed in the time period of 1925-1927. Ivanova was already involved with Filonov's Cooperative at this time when Filonov himself was producing some of his most politically engaged of anti-clerical works such as his 1925 "The Colonial Politic."
8 By 1924, many churches had had their crosses removed, left either unadorned or surmounted by the Soviet Star.
9 Julius F. Heckler, *Religion and Communism* (London: Chapman and Hall, 1933), 260.
10 The Bolsheviks' use of museums to debunk the spiritual and religious value of objects parallels the subjugation of "artifacts" from other cultures to the context of high art and ethnography, an act often perpetrated in Western museums.

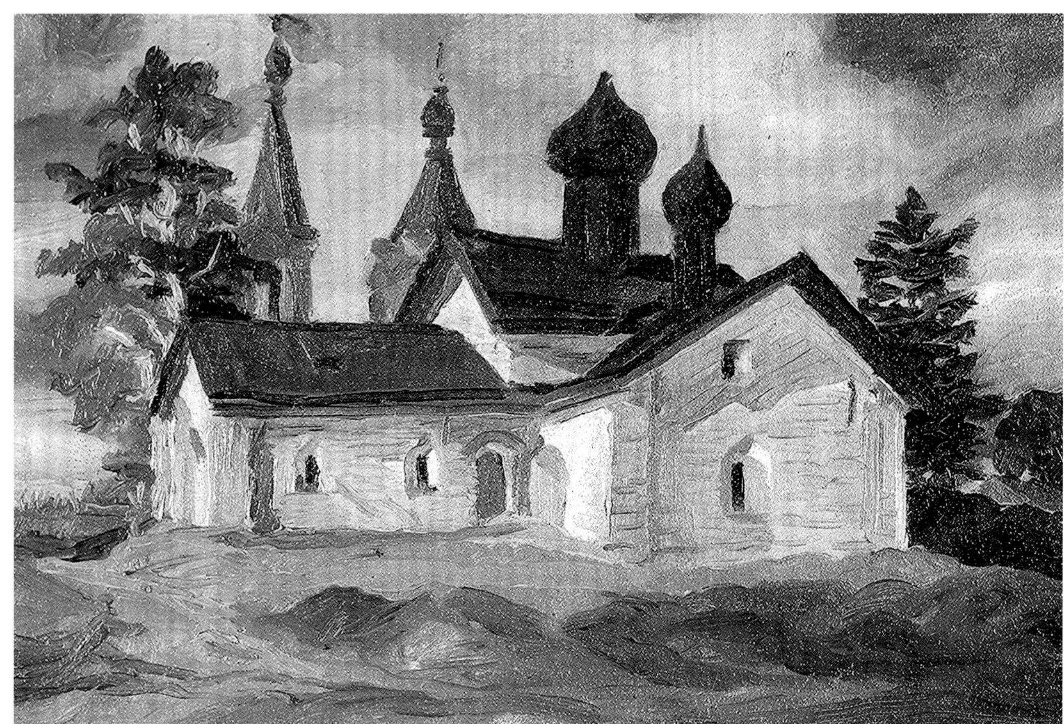

Fig. 43 Church in Courtyside
(F1) 1934-1950

vodka. Above the Priest, appears the exclamation "Down with the Rabbis! Down with the Monks!" while behind him stands a figure labeled "Matushka" (meaning both "Mother Superior" and tsarina); most likely the reference is to the Tsarina Alexandra, who was largely responsible for maintaining Rasputin's presence in the Imperial court.

The small demon in the bottom center of *Together We Will Climb*, tells the priest to take it easy; he is as common in anti-religious works as the motif of the drunken priest. For example, in the anonymous parody, *The Marriage at Cana* (fig. 42), published in the atheistic journal, *Bezboznhnik*,[11] a sickly Christ reaches for yet another drop, while devilish imps rest on the shoulders of a man vomiting and of a figure passed out on the floor—a scene reminiscent of pre-Revolutionary works such as Vasilii Perov's *Refectory* (1861, RM).

Although Ivanova did not become a career artist after graduating from the Academy, she did not abandon her interest in artistic pursuits. In the 1930s and 1940s, she returned, in a different manner, to religious subject-matter, depicting churches and monasteries within contemplative *landscapes* (cf. fig. 43, F1, fig. 9, F27, p. 31). These landscapes with their gentle churches were meant less for public consumption than as a reflection of personal sentiments. Initially, the Bolsheviks had sought to eradicate religion, but by the late 1930s Stalin needed to restore Orthodoxy so as to promote a national identity with which to combat the military threat of Fascist Germany. In any case, Ivanova's later images allow for a deeper understanding of her earlier anti-religious works. Although she was committed to the new state, joining the Communist Party in the late 1930s, she never fully divested herself of religious ideas. She felt freer to express her views of religion in her own style with a sincerity that resulted in compositions both startling and beautiful. Although, of course, Ivanova's anti-religious images were influenced by the strident ideology with which she was indoctrinated, they also reveal that in the 1920s there was still a diversity of interpretation and style. Outside the political establishment, the concept of "anti-religion" had many meanings even to those, like Ivanova, who were sincere in their enthusiasm for the new Bolshevik State and eager to enter paradise, albeit a Communist one.

11 There were many artists who produced anti-religious images in various styles, among them Deni (pseudonym of Viktor Denisov), Boris Efimov, and Dmitrii Moor.

Ivanova As Writer

MAKSIM V. KLYMENTIEV

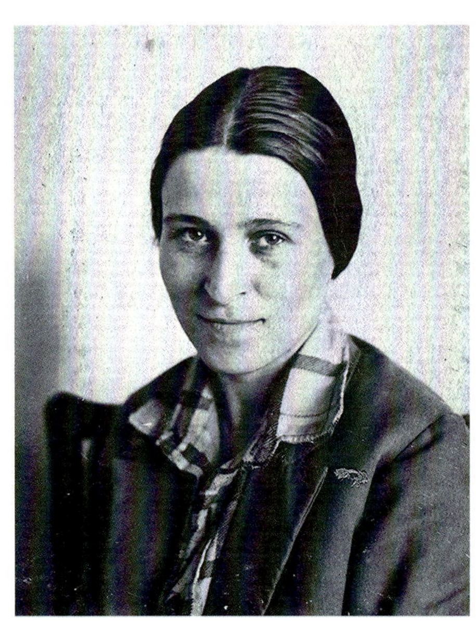

Fig. 44 Liudmila Ivanova
(G1) 1933

Liudmila Ivanova was a painter, using visual images, not words, in her creations. On the other hand, words fill the spaces between her paintings, uniting and unifying them. After all, in Russian the expression "to paint a picture" is literally "to write a picture," with the verb *pisat*, "to write." The verbal invades the visual and becomes an icon.

On one level, Ivanova herself is a metaphor for this complementary interplay inasmuch as she seemed preoccupied from the first by the tension between her artistic personality (the visual) and her documentary identification (the verbal). Ivanova's surname is the most common last name in Russia and perhaps she developed her artistic individuality precisely to counter this anonymity. Perhaps this explains her decision to lengthen her last name to "Ivanova-Tatarovich" after her first marriage in 1923 to Ignatii Tartarovich; perhaps this explains her decision to retain only the first part of that name after her divorce in 1926 until 1941, when she married her third husband, Vladislav Ravdonikas, for the second time and replaced her name with his. For an artist, a change of names generates serious repercussions; suddenly, all achievements associated with a prior name are separated and then suspended within this relocation of attribution. Ivanova must have been aware of this consequence.

The texts that Ivanova produced during her lifetime—the names of her persona, the titles of her pictures, the diaries, letters, intimate notes, bureaucratic forms duly completed, and even signatures—grant meaning to the manifest chaos whence her works have come down to us. Other texts in the IMRC bequest, written by relatives, friends, and anonymous contemporaries also address and portray her with inevitably conflicting interpretations and inconsistencies.

Ivanova lived and worked in a special time and place—the Soviet Union of the 1920s and 1930s—that made inordinate demands on the written and spoken word. The Soviet machine turned the freedom of its referential capacity into the slavery of a didactic label. The primary functions of discourse were usurped by a monster of a state that used words to speak to and for itself alone.

Ivanova hailed from a social stratum that gained particular benefit from the Russian revolutions of 1905 and October 1917—ready access to higher education, full participation in social intercourse, and engagement with an art of social and cultural purpose. Ivanova matured as an artist just when the art of Russia was in a state of suspension, i.e., when it had already fulfilled its social mandate and was operating in a new and revolutionary condition. Many of the older avant-garde artists were eager to explore this condition and to see their revolutionary dream come true—an aspiration both heroic and futile. Ivanova belonged to a new and different genera-tion for whom the momentum of the Revolution was expressed, interpreted, and rhetoricized above all, in words. The momentum provided them with a unique asset—the power to (re)name—which explains the power that, especially, the printed word exerted upon them; hence, their further fascination with the sacrificial and puni-tive role that language assumed in the Soviet Union under Stalin.

Apart from paintings, drawings, and designs, Ivanova's legacy con-tains a number of texts written at different periods of her career, including her diary and personal correspondence. There are also various official documents, memos, official forms, and permits—geographical and historical traces of her life in the shifting sands of Soviet reality. Paper was pervasive, because the state issued, multi-plied, disseminated, and verified documents as a means of measur-ing its own size and stature and of formalizing the citizen's role in the new republic. In the early 1920s, this documentary omnipres-ence manifested itself not only because the photo ID hardly exist-ed, but also as a response to the confusion of the Civil War, when people changed their names or traded identities—the verbal had to compensate for the lack of the visual. In fact, the numerous forms that the Soviet citizen had to fill out constituted the state's concept of reality as a textualized space in which the individual was required to insert his or her personal information.

Ivanova's diary and personal correspondence are revealing in this regard, especially as both genres, like the confession, presuppose a first-person narration. The difference between the three genres lies only in audience: in the case of the diary, it is the self; private corre-spondence usually addresses another; while the confession is directed toward the transcendental or transpersonal. Ivanova's first-person texts reflect her awareness of all three audiences.

Pavel Filonov, perhaps Ivanova's principal mentor, required all his students to keep diaries, his own being exemplary. Whenever he failed to communicate in everyday life, Filonov reverted to his diary, recording what his works could not. The addressee of Filonov's diary, therefore, was basically himself and at times his narrative resembles the logbook of a spaceship light-years away whose pilot records daily events—addressing himself with the knowledge that he and his words will be retrieved only after many years. Indeed, some of the Soviet avant-gardists of the 1920s—including Vladimir Maiakvosky, Filonov with his cosmic voyages, and Vladimir Tatlin with his flying "pterodactyl of the future"—entertained similar preoccupations about, and trajectories into, the future.

It is relevant to remember that in 1932-1933, while still using the methods of Analytical Art, Ivanova participated in a major project of the Filonov School—the illustration of the Russian edition of the *Kalevala*. In this context, she was obliged to visualize a verbal art that had survived for many centuries solely through the agency of the spoken word. Ivanova and her colleagues had to reproduce linguistic shifts registered in language on a most basic level—in prepositions. This process involved the transposition of the linguis-tic material as it existed in the text (in a closed form) and into pictures, i.e., opening the borders with which the text demarcates itself. The contamination of the visual by the verbal resulted in the iconicized drawings that illustrate not so much the epic text as the state of the ancient Finnish literary language.

Unfortunately, the Ivanova archive does not contain her diary entries for the late 1920s and very early 1930s when she was close to Filonov and was involved in preparations for the *Kalevala*. But even the fragment that has survived is revealing, for the words are directed at different addressees—herself, a generic reader, and her beloved, Vladislav Ravdonikas (she even sent him parts of her diary in letter form). In form and destination, the shadow of Filonov looms large in the Ivanova diary, but the fact that the addressee was not her teacher may also indicate a wish to escape his influence.

One of the most distinct characteristics of diary writing is the imme-
diacy with which it records daily events, something characteristic of
Ivanova's diary, where she makes daily records of experience:

> I am working softly, quietly, and lovingly. Working with the
> discipline of stone is like nothing else. Working on paper, you
> usually make some irresponsible scrawl and maintain a rather
> desultory attitude towards the work. But stone, like a magnet,
> draws one stroke after another out of you… Every movement
> of the hand is accountable. Because when you have drawn a
> line on this kind of surface, you can't erase it… Working on my
> fourth picture, I've begun to sense my freedom and, despite
> the fact that my hand is still not entirely mobile, I sense a
> freedom with stone as with paper.[1]

In her diary, Ivanova often slips into a verbal delineation of her
artistic methods and working techniques, for example, what she
calls "painterly concentration:" "Oh, how I want to paint!…. Every
sign of firmness and certainty of eye and hand is a joy for me."[2] An
entry written several days later "localizes" her desire to paint:
"Myriad thoughts, myriad desires, I am being drawn to the canvas.
The smell of paints in the room. It excites me, it whets my desire to
sit down and start working."[3] Other entries analyze the finished
work via description of various categories that she has elaborated.
For example, one of her Crimean landscapes elicits the following
verbal response: "I drew painting from the sketch that I had from
inside the canyon, a view of Cherkes-Kermen in the mountains.
I gave it a very solid composition. I did everything directly with the
brush. All the colors have been laid down, all the forms are clean
cut. Light and shadow, everything is in place. Suede hillsides with
dazzling, white cliffs in the foreground, although still without the
small houses, in a remarkable interplay of light and color."[4] A week
later, she describes the final stage of the painting, a procedure
reminiscent of her apprenticeship to Filonov (who recorded in detail
how many hours he worked on such and such a day): "The weekend
of 18th I again painted from 10:00 a.m. to 4:00 p.m. and then,
after lunch, from 4:30 to 6:00 p.m."[5] This picture, painted over an
earlier painting in Filonov's style, was Ivanova's first major work

after her break with Filonov and its symbolic significance is clear.
Another, more objective reason for the recurrence of this landscape
in her diary is that she could not remember the actual color of the
Crimean sky. Perhaps by focusing on the sky, the "celestial" part of
her breakaway painting, she wished to counter the darkness of
her Filonovian underpainting: "The canvas is in front of me," she
wrote, "The sky troubles me. I want to paint."[6] In contradistinction
to Filonov's works, almost always devoid of sky, the sky came to
play an ever increasing role in Ivanova's later works.

Fig. 45 Profile of Woman Looking Up
(D17) 1922

1 L. Ivanova diary, 24 September 1934 call no. G94, IMRC.
2 Ibid, 10 September 1934.
3 Ibid, 14 September 1934.
4 Ibid, 12 September 1934.
5 Ibid, 20 September 1934.
6 Ibid, 14 September 1934.

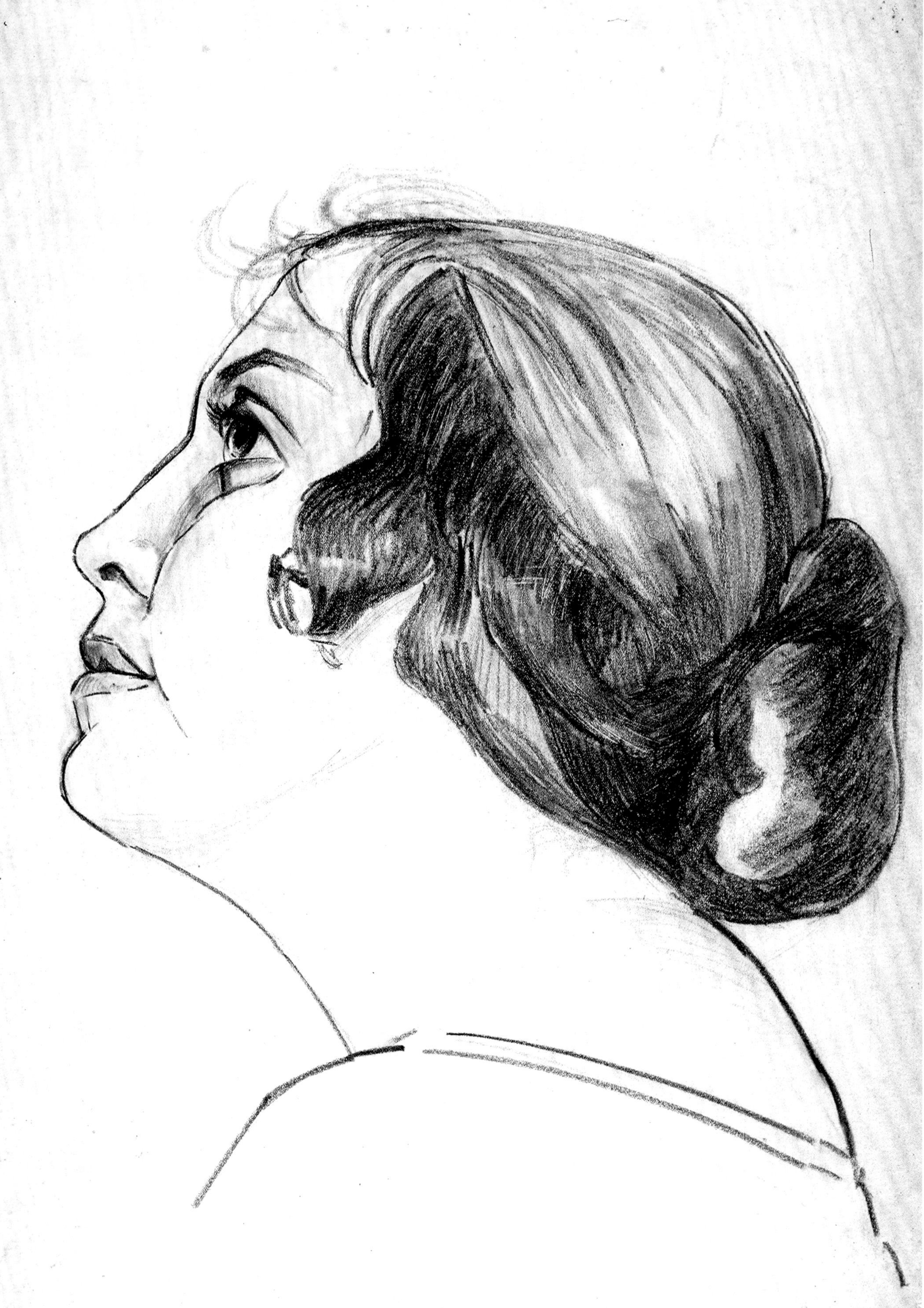

Glossary of Terms and Acronyms

JOHN E. BOWLT

Academy of Arts: Academy of Fine Arts, St. Petersburg/Petrograd/ Leningrad. Founded in 1757, Catherine the Great was its first president. Between 1918 and 1921, the Academy was replaced by Svomas (q.v.); in the 1920s, it was also referred to as Vkhutemas (q.v.).

AIMK: Academy of the History of Material Culture (Akademiia istorii materialnoi kultury), Petrograd/Leningrad, 1919-1937.

Collective of Masters of Analytical Art: Kollektiv masterov analiticheskogo iskusstva. Group of Leningrad artists founded by Pavel Filonov in 1925 that supported his theory of Universal Flowering and Analytical Art. At various times, the group included such painters, graphic artists and sculptors as Tatiana Glebova, Liudmila Ivanova, Evgenii Kibrik, and Alisa Poret. Continued until 1932 when, along with other art societies and associations, it was banned by government decree. The collective's most important productions include a design for a production of *Revizor* (1927) and an illustrated edition of the *Kalevala* (1933).

Comintern: Communist International. Unification of Communist Parties worldwide through debate and convocation; Tatlin designed his famous Tower for the III International in Moscow in 1919.

Erste russische Kunstausstellung: First Russian Art Exhibition. First major exhibition of Soviet art held abroad (at the Galerie Van Diemen, Berlin in 1922), it also traveled to Amsterdam in modified form. Although the avant-garde was well represented, this commercial exhibition was a survey of many trends.

Exhibition of Paintings by Petrograd Artists of All Directions: Broad survey of new trends organized in Petrograd in 1923. Among the many contributors were Ilia Chashnik, Pavel Filonov, Pavel Mansurov, and Vladimir Tatlin.

Ginkhuk: State Institute of Artistic Culture (Gosudarstvennyi institut khudozhestvennnoi kultury). Petrograd/Leningrad counterpart to Inkhuk (q.v.); developed from the Petrograd affiliation of the Museums of Artistic Culture (q.v.) in 1923 (ratified 1924) and contained five basic departments: 1) Department of Form and Theory headed by Kazimir Malevich; 2) Department of Material Culture headed by Vladimir Tatlin (1922-1925); 3) Department of Organic Culture headed by Mikhail Matiushin; 4) Department of Experimentation headed by Pavel Mansurov; 5) Department of General Ideology headed by Pavel Filonov (later by Nikolai Punin).

IMRC: Institute of Modern Russian Culture, University of Southern California, Los Angeles.

Inkhuk: Institute of Artistic Culture (Institut khudozhestvennoi kultury). Founded as a research institute in Moscow in 1920 with Vasilii Kandinsky as it first president. With affiliations in Petrograd, Vitebsk, and other cities, Inkhuk's membership included many avant-garde artists. Active through 1924.

IZO: The Visual Arts (Izobrazitelnye iskusstva). The Visual Arts Section of NKP (q.v.) founded in 1918 under David Shterenberg. IZO was responsible for art exhibitions, official commissions, art institutes, art education, etc. At first, many of the avant-garde were involved in its activities.

Jack of Diamonds: Group organized by Mikhail Larionov in Moscow in 1910 and initially supported by many radical artists, including Natalia Goncharova and Kazimir Malevich. After the first exhibition in Moscow in 1910-1911, the group split into two factions, one, led by Larionov, gave rise to the Donkey's Tail; the other was led by Robert Falk, Petr Konchalovsky, Aristarkh Lentulov, Ilia Mashkov et al. The Jack of Diamonds organized regular exhibitions in Moscow and St. Petersburg between 1910 and 1917, some of them international in scope.

Komsmol: Communist Youth Organization (Kommmunisticheskii Soiuz molodezhi).

LOSKh: Leningrad Organization of the Union of Artists of the RSFSR (Leningradskaia organizatsiia Soiuza khudozhnikov RSFSR).

Lubok: A cheap, handcolored print or broadsheet often depicting allegorical and satirical scenes from Russian life. The bright colors and crude outlines of the lubok attracted many twentieth century Russian artists.

Museums of Painterly Culture: Network of Museums of Painterly (also called Artistic or Plastic) Culture established for Moscow, Petrograd, and other cities in 1919. Natan Altman, Vasilii Kandinsky, Alexander Rodchenko, and other avant-garde artists helped organize this network, whose purpose was to collect works by modern Russian artists; its most important Museum functioned in Moscow from 1919 to 1924.

Narkompros: People's Commissariat for Enlightenment (Narodnyi komissariat prosveshcheniia). Established under Anatolii Lunacharsky just after the Revolution, this radical Ministry of Culture opened various subsections responsible for the arts, e.g., IZO (q.v.), TEO (Theater), and MUZO (Music).

NEP: New Economic Policy (Novaia ekonimcheskaia politika). Instituted by Lenin in 1921 in the wake of the October Revolution and its attendant chaos, NEP allowed a partial return to the free enterprise system in order to revive trade and investment and to bolster the production of essential commodities. Replaced by the First Five Year Plan in 1928, NEP canceled the following year.

RM: See Russian Museum (in pictorial and bibliographic references).

RSFSR: Russian Soviet Federative Socialist Republic (Rossiiskaia Sovetskaia Federativnaia Sotsialisticheskaia Respublika).

Russian Museum: Principal collection of Russian art in St. Petersburg. Founded in 1898 as the Alexander III Russian Museum.

Socialist Realism: Didactic, narrative style of art that emphasized advocacy of, and allegiance to, the political ideology of the Soviet régime; officially sanctioned from 1932, Socialist Realism dominated Soviet painting, literature, and music until the 1970s.

Svomas: Free State Art Studios (Svobodnye gosudarstvennye khudozhestvennye masterskie). In 1918, the Moscow Institute of Painting, Sculpture and Architecture and the Stroganov Institute were merged to form Svomas; leading art schools in other major cities, including the Academy of Arts, Petrograd, were also removed. In 1920, however, Svomas, Moscow, was renamed Vkhutemas (q.v.) and the Academy in Petrograd was reinstated. Many avant-garde artists, including Ivan Kliun, Liubov Popova, Alexander Rodchenko, and Vladimir Tatlin, contributed to the radical pedagogical and administrative developments that accompanied these reorganizations.

TG: Tretiakov Gallery (q.v.) (in pictorial and bibliographic references).

Tretiakov Gallery: Principal Moscow collection of Russian art, founded in 1892 on the basis of the collection of Pavel Tretiakov, a Moscow businessman.

Union of Youth: Group of artists, critics, and esthetes established by Vladimir Markov, Olga Rozanova, Uisif Shkolnik et al. in St. Petersburg in 1910. Published an art journal under the same name (1912-1913) and sponsored a series of exhibitions between 1910 and 1914 to which many of the avant-garde contributed, including David Burliuk, Pavel Filonov, Mikhail Larionov, and Ivan Puni.

Vkhutein: Higher State Art-Technical Institute (Vysshii gosudarstvennyi khudozhestvenno-tekhnicheskii institut). Vkhutein replaced Vkhutemas (q.v.) in 1926 and was replaced by the Moscow Institute of Visual Arts in 1930.

Vkhutemas: Higher State Art-Technical Studios (Vysshie gosudarstvennye khudozhestvenno-tekhnicheskie masterskie). Replaced Svomas (q.v.) in 1920 and was replaced by Vkhutein (q.v.) in 1926. Although the Moscow Vkhutemas is the most famous, the name was also applied to other art schools, such as, the reinstated Academy of Arts in Petrograd/Leningrad.

Vsekokhudozhnik: All-Russian Cooperative Association "Art" (Vserossiiskoe kooperativnoe tovarishchestvo "Khudozhnik"). Founded in Moscow in 1934 as an artists' trade union with exhibition and publishing facilities; discontinued with the establishment of the Union of Artists of the USSR in 1939.

World of Art: Group of St. Petersburg artists, critics, and aesthetes founded by Alexandre Benois, Sergei Diaghilev et al. in the late 1890s. Published an art journal under the same name (1898-1904) and sponsored a series of exhibitions (1899-1906) to propagate contemporary art; revived as an exhibition society from 1910 to 1924.

Zor-ved (See-Know): Title of Matiushin's sensory system which incorporated both expanded sight and prior knowledge and cognition to produce a more comprehensive perception of reality. Coming to the concept in the 1910s, Mikhail Matiushin and then his students (especially the Ender family) elaborated the theory in the 1920s.

Selected Bibliography of English Language Sources Relevant to Liudmila Ivanova and the Leningrad Avant-Garde

Richard Andrews and Milena Kalinovska, eds. *Art into Life. Russian Constructivism 1914-1932*. Ex. cat. Seattle, WA: Henry Art Gallery, University of Washington; New York: Rizzoli, 1990. Exhibition also at the Walker Art Gallery, Minneapolis.

Stephanie Barron and Maurice Tuchman, eds. *The Avant-Garde in Russia 1910-1930. New Perspectives*. Ex. cat. Los Angeles: Los Angeles County Museum of Art; Cambridge, MA: MIT Press, 1980.

John E. Bowlt, ed. and trans. *Russian Art of the Avant-Garde: Theory and Criticism 1902-1934*. London: Thames and Hudson, 1988.

John E. Bowlt and Matthew Drutt, eds. *Amazonen der Avantgarde. Amazons of the Avant-Garde*. Ex. cat. Berlin: Deutsche Guggenheim, 1999. Exhibition also at the Royal Academy, London; Peggy Guggenheim Museum, Venice; Guggenheim Museum, Bilbao; Solomon R. Guggenheim Museum, New York.

John E. Bowlt and Nicoletta Misler. *The Thyssen-Bornemisza Collection. Twentieth-Century Russian and East European Painting*. London: Zwemmer, 1993.

Charlotte Douglas. *Swans of Other Worlds: Kazimir Malevich and the Origins of Abstraction in Russia*. Ann Arbor, MI: UMI Research Press, 1980.

Camilla Gray. *The Great Experiment. Russian Art 1863-1922*. London: Thames and Hudson, 1962.

Mikhail Guerman. *Art of the October Revolution*. New York: Abrams, 1979.

Jürgen Harten and Evgenija Petrowa, eds. *Pavel Filonov und seine Schule*. Ex. cat. Köln: Dumont, 1990. Exhibition at the Kunsthalle, Düsseldorf.

Jeremy Howard. *The Union of Youth: An Artists' Society of the Russian Avant-Garde*. Manchester, New York: Manchester University Press, 1992.

Gerald Janecek. *The Look of Russian Literature. Avant-Garde Visual Experiments 1900-1930*. Princeton: Princeton University Press, 1984.

Anna Kafetsi, ed. *Russian Avant-Garde 1910-1930. The George Costakis Collection*. Catalog of exhibition at the National Gallery and Alexandros Soutzos Museum, Athens, 1996 (two volumes).

Christina Lodder. *Russian Constructivism*. New Haven: Yale University Press, 1983.

Nicoletta Misler and John E. Bowlt. *Pavel Filonov: A Hero and His Fate*. Austin, TX: Silvergirl, 1983.

Karen Myers. *Liudmila Alexandrovna Ivanova (1904-1978)*. The Knowing Eye. Ex. cat. Los Angeles: Institute of Modern Russian Culture, 1990.

Evgenia Petrova and Irina Karasik. *New Art for a New Era: Malevich's vision of the Russian avant-garde from the collection of the State Russian Museum, St. Petersburg*. Ex. cat. London: Booth-Cliborn Editions, 1999. Exhibition at Barbican Art Gallery, London.

Alla Povelikhina, ed. *Matjuschin und die Leningrader Avantgarde*. Ex. cat. Stuttgart: Oktogon, 1991. Exhibition at the Zentrum für Kunst und Medientechnologie, Karlsruhe.

Gail Harrison Roman and Virginia Hagelstein Marquardt, eds. *The Avant-Garde Frontier: Russia Meets the West, 1910-1930*. Gainesville, FL: University Press of Florida, 1992.

Margit Rowell and Angelica Zander Rudenstine, eds. *Art of the Avant-garde in Russia: Selections from the George Costakis Collection*. Ex. cat. New York: Solomon R. Guggenheim Museum, 1981.

Angelica Rudenstine, ed. *Russian Avant-Garde Art. The George Costakis Collection*. New York: Abrams, 1981.

The Great Utopia: the Russian and Soviet Avant-Garde, 1915-1932. Ex. cat. New York: Solomon R. Guggenheim Museum, 1992. Exhibition also at the State Tretiakov Gallery, Moscow; State Russian Museum, St. Petersburg; Schirn Kunsthalle, Frankfurt; Stedelijk Museum, Amsterdam.

Myuda Yablonskaya. *Women Artists of Russia's New Age 1900-1935*. London: Thames and Hudson, 1990.

Checklist of the Exhibition

Notes to Readers

1. All works are by the artist Liudmila Ivanova unless otherwise indicated.
2. All works have been lent by the Institute of Modern Russian Culture at the University of Southern California, Los Angeles, unless otherwise noted. Catalog numbers have been assigned by the IMRC.
3. All dimensions are given first in inches (in.) and then in centimeters (cm), height preceding width.
4. Unless otherwise noted, all other attributions and dates have been added collectively by the curatorial and administrative team.

Early Works (1921-1926)

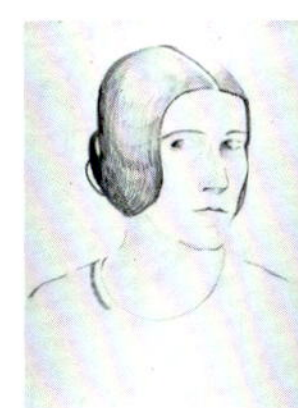

Woman with Gaze Askance
Pencil on paper
27 4/5 x 20 4/5 in. (70.5 x 52.8 cm)
1922
B3

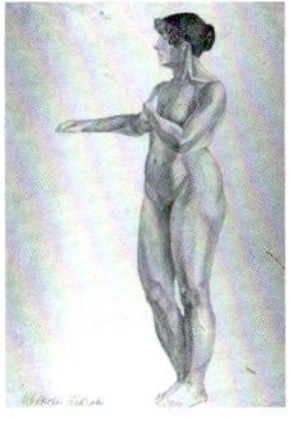

Standing Female Nude: Three-Quarter View
Pencil on paper
28 2/5 x 21 1/5 in. (71.0 x 53.0 cm)
Signed: "Ivanova Tatarovich"
Verso: Unfinished version of the same subject
c. 1921-1924
B4

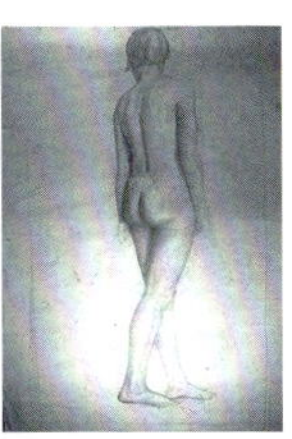

Back View of Nude with Crossed Legs
Pencil on paper
28 1/5 x 21 in. (70.5 x 55.5 cm)
Signed: "Toskin" in red on recto, in pencil on verso
c. 1921-1924
B5

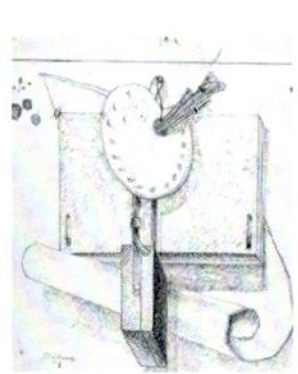

Artist's Tools
Sepia ink on paper
14 1/10 x 13 1/10 in. (35.2 x 32.7 cm)
Signed: "L. Ivanova" lower left
1922
B6

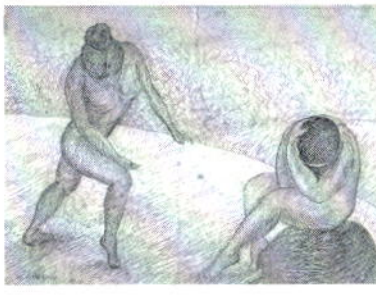

Two Nudes
Sepia ink on paper
13 1/10 x 15 4/5 in. (32.8 x 39.5 cm)
Signed and dated: "L. Ivanova 1922"
1922
B7

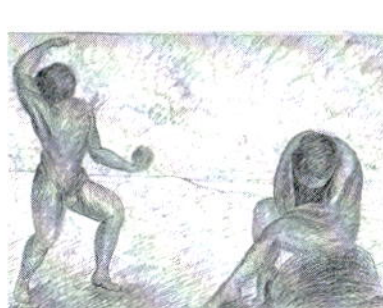

Man with Hunched Figure
Sepia ink on paper
13 1/10 x 15 9/10 in. (32.8 x 39.7 cm)
Signed and dated: "L. Ivanova 1922"
1922
B8

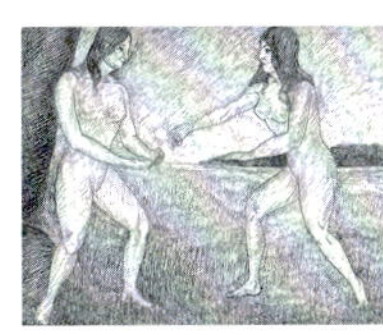

Meeting
Sepia and ink on paper
13 1/10 x 19 9/10 in. (32.8 x 49.8 cm)
Signed: "L. Ivanova"
Inscription: "vstrecha" (meeting) lower left
Verso: Stylized female figure pencil sketch
1922
B9

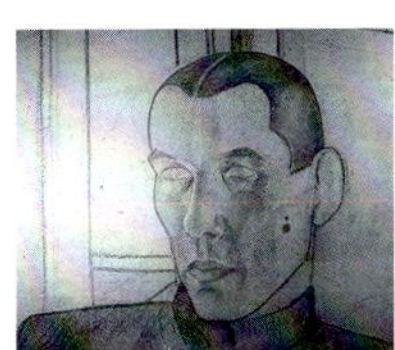

Man with Parted Hair
Pencil on paper
20 3/5 x 24 in. (51.5 x 60.0 cm)
Verso shaded over in pencil
1922
B10

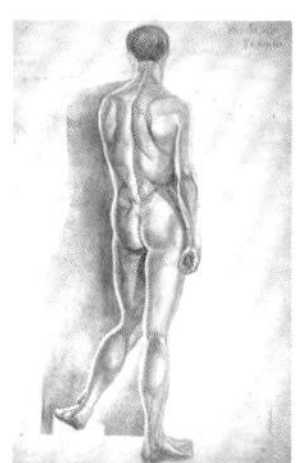

Back View of Male Nude with Bent Left Knee
Pencil on paper
27 2/5 x 19 1/10 in. (68.4 x 47.8 cm)
Signed: "Ivanova Liudm."
Inscription: "IV K. Zhiv. Fak" (4th course of
Painting Faculty)
1922
B12

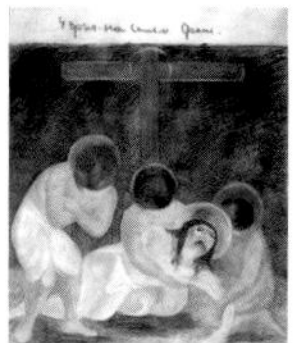

Four Figures on a Blue Background
Pastel on paper
23 1/5 x 20 2/5 in. (58.0 x 51.0 cm)
Inscription: "4 fig. na sinem fone." (4 figures on
a blue background) above the composition
c. 1923
B13
Conservation supported by Ronald & Roxanne
Meyer

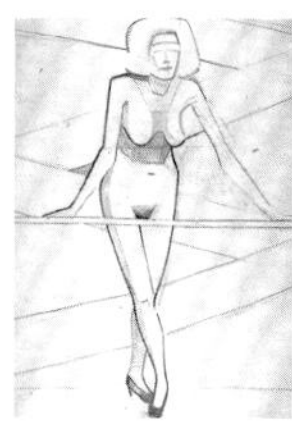

Female Nude with High-Heels
Pencil on paper
24 4/5 x 19 1/5 in. (62.0 x 48.0 cm)
1922-1926
B14

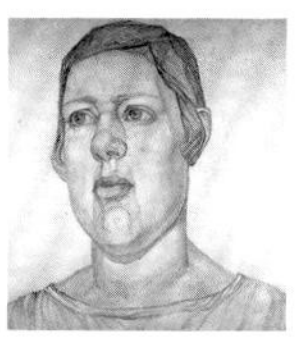

Frontal Female Portrait from Low Angle
Pencil on paper
20 2/5 x 20 in. (51.0 x 50.0 cm)
Signed: Ivanova Tatarovich
1924-1925
B15

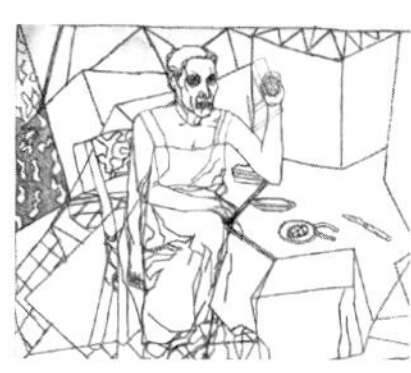

Woman at Table Holding Glass
Ink and pencil on paper
12 7/10 x 14 2/5 in. (31.7 x 35.9 cm)
1925-1926
C1

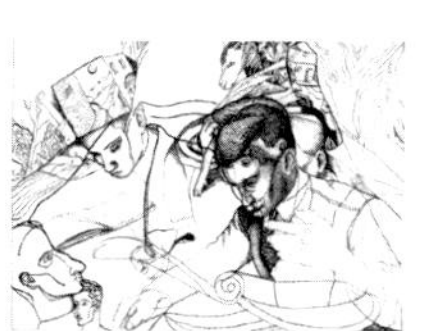

The Writer
Ink and pencil on paper
9 9/10 x 13 2/5 in. (24.7 x 33.6 cm)
Mounting tabs on upper verso corner
1925-1927
C5

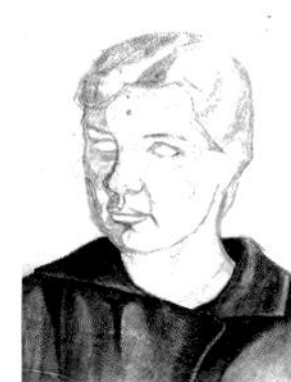

Woman in Dark Dress
Charcoal and pencil on paper
24 7/10 x 20 2/5 in. (61.7 x 51.0 cm)
1922
C8

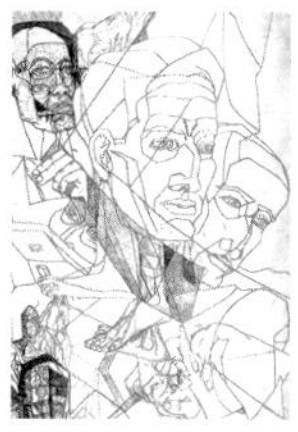

Heads, Hands, and Feet
Pencil and ink on paper
29 2/5 x 21 3/10 in. (73.5 x 53.3 cm)
1925-1927
C10

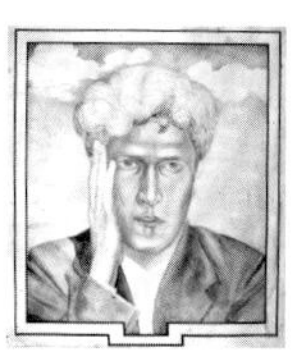

Portrait of Man with Clouds
Ink, ink wash, pencil, and watercolor on paper
19 3/5 x 18 in. (49.0 x 45.0 cm)
1925
C12

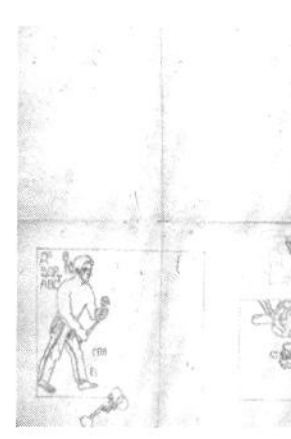

Long Live the Power of the Soviets
Pencil on paper
17 4/5 x 14 2/5 in. (44.4 x 36.0 cm)
Inscription: "Da zdravst vlast sone…" (Long live
the power of the sone…)
Verso: Drawing of man drinking water
1924-1926
C13

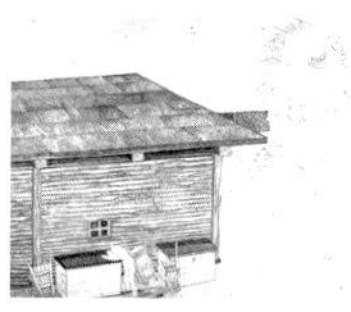

Shed from High Vantage Point
Pencil and ink on paper
21 3/5 x 29 1/10 in. (54.0 x 72.7 cm)
1925
C14

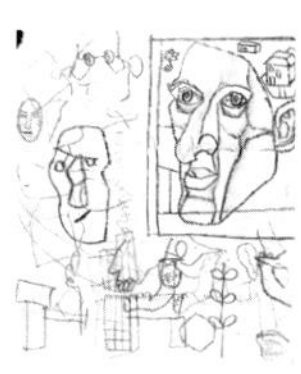

Freehand Sketches of Face
Pencil on paper
6 3/10 x 6 4/5 in. (15.7 x 17.0 cm)
1924
C17

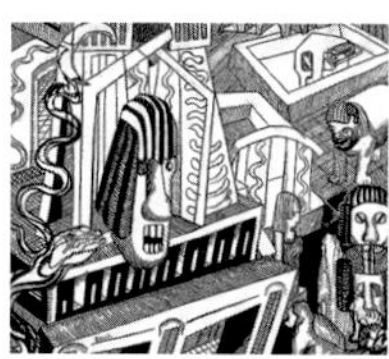

Serpents and Idols
Ink on cardboard
5 2/5 x 6 1/5 in. (13.5 x 15.6 cm)
1926
C18

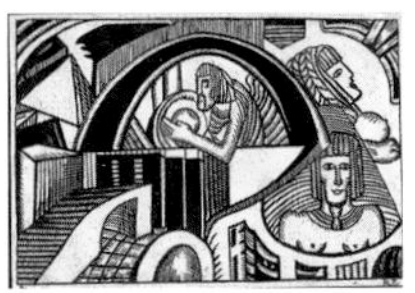

Design with Egyptian Motifs
Black ink on paper mounted on cardboard
5 7/10 x 7 2/5 in. (14.3 x 18.4 cm)
Signed: "L. I. T."
1926
C19

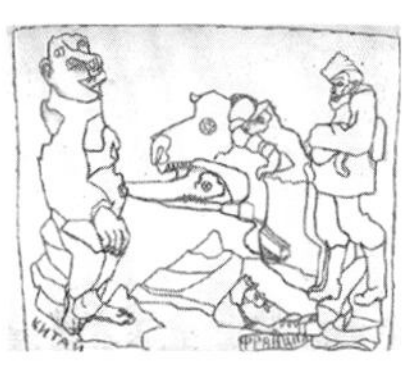

Between China and France
Pencil and watercolor on paper
6 1/10 x 7 2/5 in. (15.3 x 18.3 cm)
Inscription: "kitai" (China) and "frantsiia"
(France) within the image on left and right,
respectively.
Verso sketches
1925-1926
C21

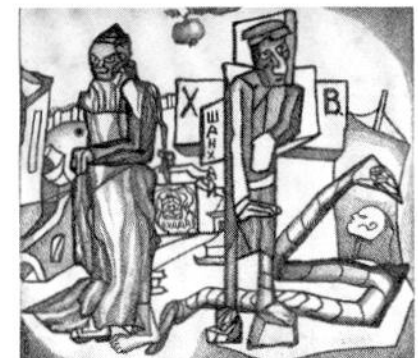

Christ is Risen
Ink and pencil on paper
5 2/5 x 6 in. (13.5 x 15.0 cm)
Dated: 1925
1925
C22
Inscription: "KhV" (Christ is Risen)
Shankhai (Shanghai)
Conservation supported by Ronald & Roxanne
Meyer

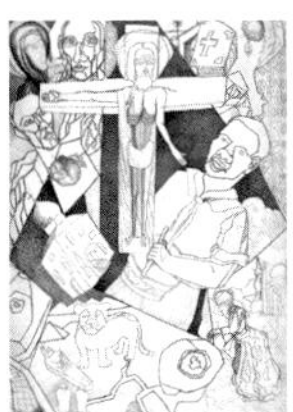

Crucifixion with Pioneer Boy
Watercolor, pencil, and ink on paper
10 7/10 x 7 7/10 in. (26.8 x 19.5 cm)
1925-1927
C23

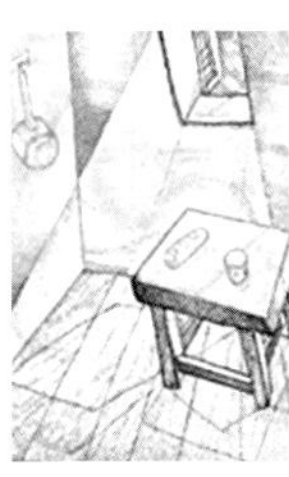

Kitchen Scene
Watercolor on paper mounted on cardboard
7 2/5 x 3 3/5 in. (18.3 x 13.9 cm)
Signed and dated: "L. A. Ivanova 1926"o
Inscription: "Poluchil Oleg Khakhenov, ot P
Ravdonikas 11.V.67 g (B Ivanova)" (Received by
Oleg Khakhenov, From P. Ravdonikas 11.5.67 (B.
Ivanova))
1926
C27

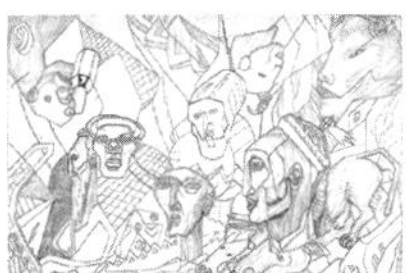

Sphinx with Central Asian Head
Pencil on paper
6 9/10 x 10 3/10 in. (17.4 x 25.7 cm)
Verso: Architectural drawing of bridge
1925-1926
C30

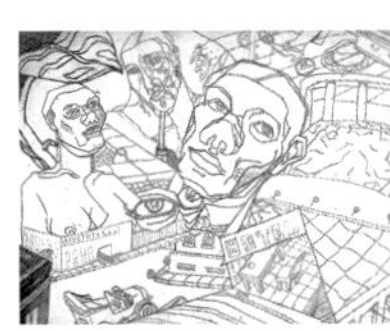

Prostitution
Pencil and watercolor on paper
9 x 11 3/5 in. (22.5 x 29.0 cm)
Inscription: "Prostitutsiia" (Prostitution) within
the image of one of the buildings
1925-1926
C31

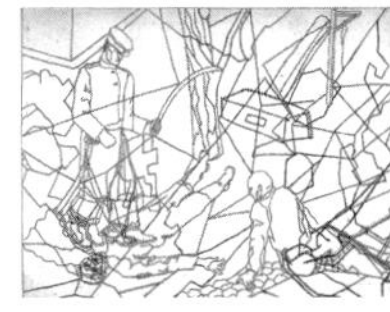

Soldier Trampling Bodies
Ink and pencil on paper
9 x 11 3/5 in. (22.5 x 29.0 cm)
1925-1926
C34

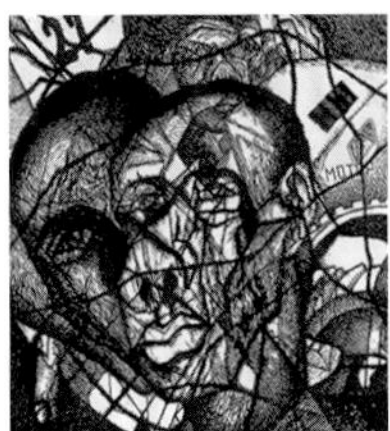

27: Heads
Ink on paper mounted on cardboard
9 1/10 x 8 3/10 in. (22.8 x 20.8 cm)
Signed and dated: "Liudm. Ivanova 1925"
1925
C36

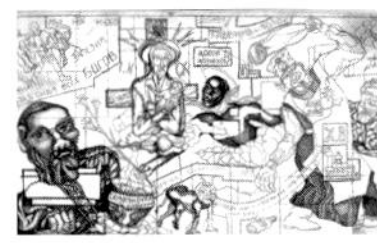

Together, We Will Climb Up to Heaven and
Chase Out All the Gods
Ink and pencil on cardboard
6 1/5 x 11 in. (15.5 x 27.4 cm)
All inscriptions are within the image clockwise
from upper left:
1. "my na nebo zalezim raz gonim vsekh bogov"
(Together, We will climb up to heaven and
chase out all the Gods)
2. "INSKh" (INRI)
3. "Doloi Ravvinov i popov, doloi monakhov"
(Down with the Rabbis and Priests, Down with
the Monks)
4. "Aliluiia" (Alleluia)
5. "Kh V" (Christ is Risen)
6. "Matushka" (Mamma or Mother)
7. "Gospodin pop–otdokhnite khot nemnozhechko
ustal uzhe" (Mr. Priest, rest just a little you are
already tired)
8. "vodka" (vodka)
9. "vkusnaia udivitelno alliluiia"
(Surprisingly tasty, Alleluia)
10. "Samogonochka usladitelnaia"
(Sweetened Moonshine)
11. "Rublia" (Rubles)
1925-1926
C37

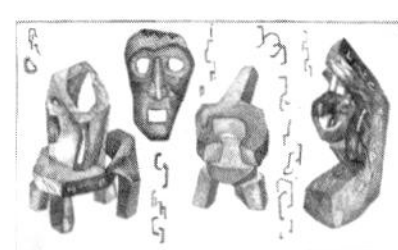

Four Objects and Cryptic Writing
Watercolor and ink on paper
5 2/5 x 9 3/10 in. (13.4 x 23.2 cm)
Signed: "Liudm. Ivanova"
Dated: Began July 1925, completed January 1927
Verso sketches
July 1925 – January 1927
C38

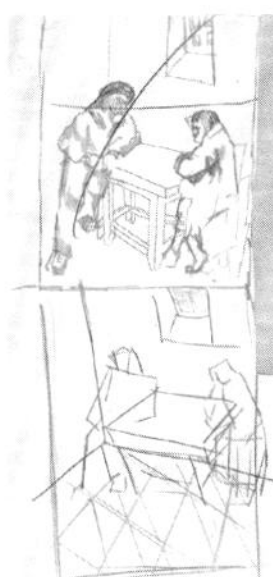

Studies for Kitchen Scene
Pencil on paper
10 3/10 x 13 9/10 in. (34.8 x 25.5 cm)
Verso: Architectural study
1926
C42

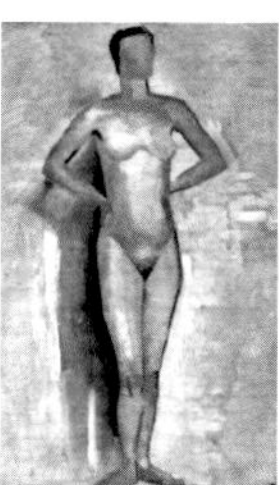

Boy in Black Trunks
Oil on paper
27 2/5 x 22 in. (68.5 x 55.0 cm)
Signed: "Ivanova Liud"
1924
D1

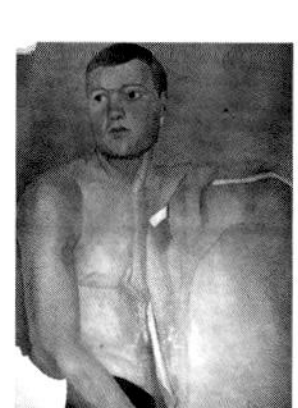

Frontal Female Nude with Hands on Hips
Oil on canvas
28 5/16 x 18 3/16 in. (71.9 x 46.2 cm)
1924
D2

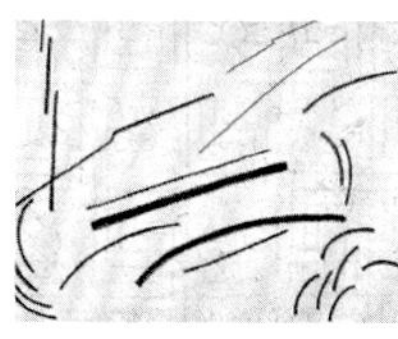

Lines and Crescents
Ink on paper
2 4/5 x 3 7/10 in. (7.0 x 9.2 cm)
Inscription on verso: "kakoe kolichestvo studen-
chestva gor Moskvy chlenov soiuza i voobshche
kolichestva vsego studenchestva po Moskve
Pervoe tvoe uvlechenie" (How many students of
the city of Moscow are members of the union and
in general how many students are there in Moscow.
Your First Sweetheart.)
1924
D3

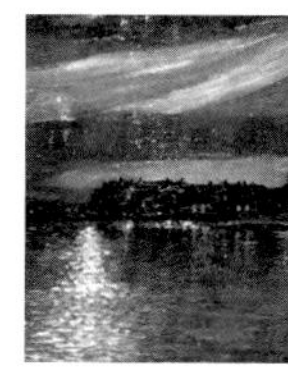

Academy of Arts, Petrograd, at Night
Oil on cardboard
8 3/10 x 7 in. (20.5 x 17.5 cm)
Signed: "L. I."
Dated: 25 September 1921
September 25, 1921
D4

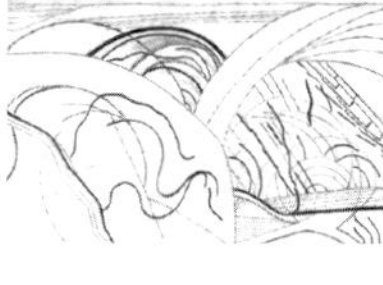

Intersecting Circles and Organic Lines
Pencil on paper
3 7/10 x 5 4/5 in. (9.3 x 14.5 cm)
1924
D5

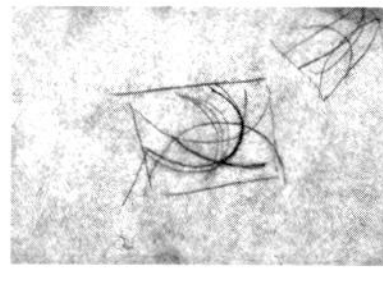

Linear Study for Figural Composition
Pencil on paper
7 4/5 x 5 3/10 in. (19.5 x 13.3 cm)
Page from Sketchbook (Golubova, Pelegeia)
Inscription: "Ded V Sini, Golubova Pelegeia"
on sketchbook
1922
D6.2

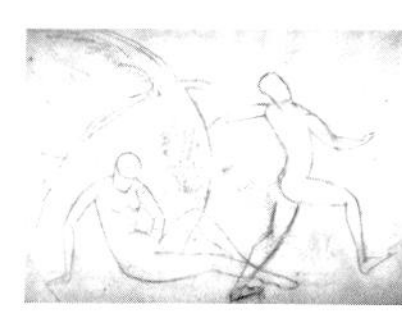

Study of Two Figures
Pencil on paper
7 4/5 x 5 3/10 in. (19.5 x 13.3 cm)
Page from sketchbook (Golubova, Pelegeia)
1922
D6.3

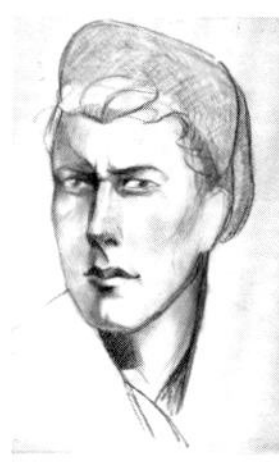

Portrait of Person with Cap
Charcoal on paper
17 3/5 x 12 1/2 in. (44.0 x 31.2 cm)
1924
D10

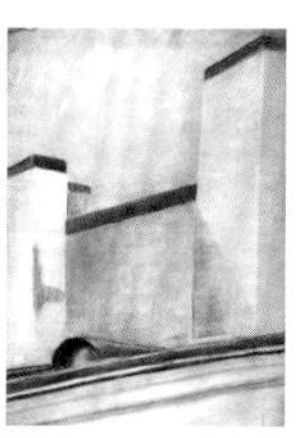

Geometric Rooftop Study
Pastel on paper
18 1/2 x 13 1/10 in. (46.3 x 32.8 cm)
1920s
D15
Conservation supported by Juliet Der Avanessian

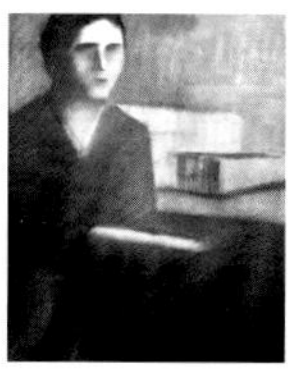

Woman in Blue
Pastel on paper
15 x 13 1/10 in. (37.5 x 32.8 cm)
1920s
D16

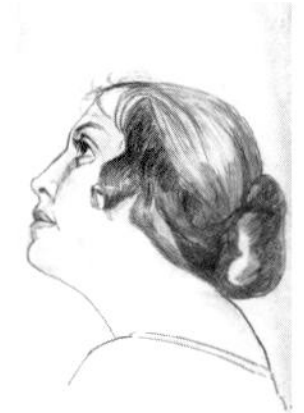

Profile of Woman Looking Up
Pencil on paper
15 4/5 x 13 1/10 in. (39.6 x 32.8 cm)
1922
D17

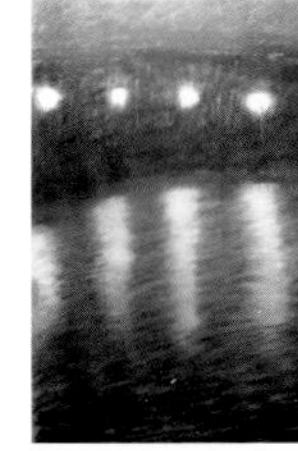

Four Lights Reflected in Water at Night
Oil pastel on paper
18 2/5 x 13 1/5 in. (46.0 x 33.0 cm)
Mid 1920s
F17

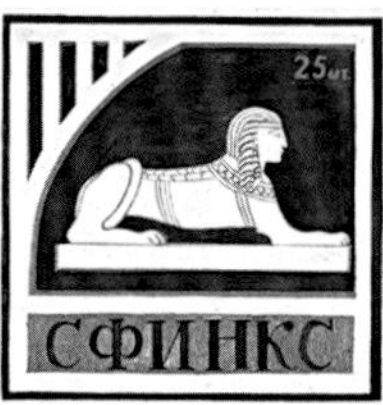

Design for Sphinx Cigarette Packaging
Gouache on cardboard
4 3/5 x 5 2/5 in. (11.5 x 13.4 cm)
Signed: "L. Ivanova"
Dated: January 18, 1926
Verso: Pencil drawing
Logo of the Academy of Arts Manufacturing Sector
January 18, 1926
E1

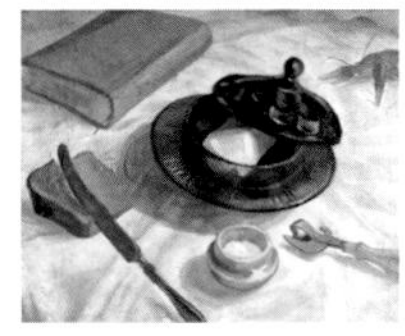

Still Life with Bread and Butter
Oil on canvas
15 1/2 x 19 2/5 in. (39.5 x 48.5 cm)
Mid 1920s
F47

Middle Works (1926-1934)

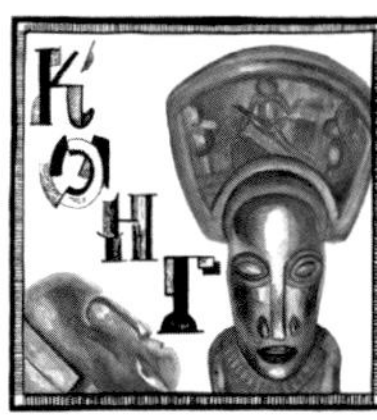

Design for Congo Cigarette Packaging
Ink and watercolor on cardboard
4 3/5 x 5 2/5 in. (11.6 x 13.5 cm)
Signed: "l. Ivanova"
Dated: January 18, 1926
Logo of the Academy of Arts
Manufacturing Sector
January 18, 1926
E2

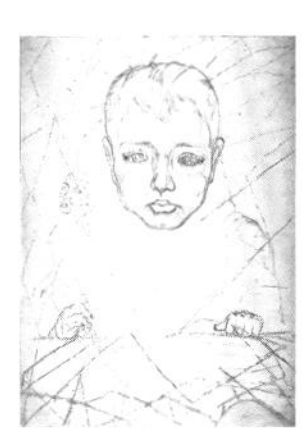

Child Holding Pencil (Son Vladimir?)
Pencil on paper
13 9/10 x 10 3/10 in. (34.8 x 25.7 cm)
1927
C2

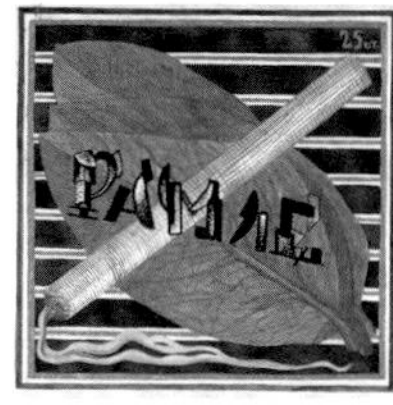

Design for Ramses Cigarettes
Gouache on cardboard
4 2/5 x 5 2/5 in. (11.1 x 13.4 cm)
Signed: "L. Ivanova"
Dated: January 18, 1926
Logo of the Academy of Arts Manufacturing
Sector
January 18, 1926
E3

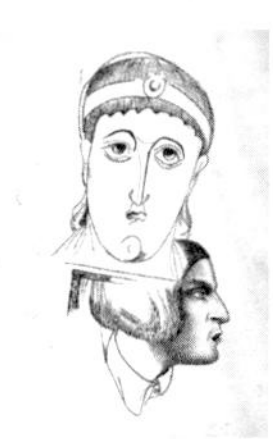

Two Heads: Frontal Byzantine Superimposed Over Modern Profile
Ink and pencil on cardboard
7 2/5 x 5 1/2 in. (18.6 x 13.7 cm)
Signed: "Liudmila Ivanova" in a variety of styles on verso (practicing her signature?)
Verso: Freehand ink sketch
1931-1933
C15

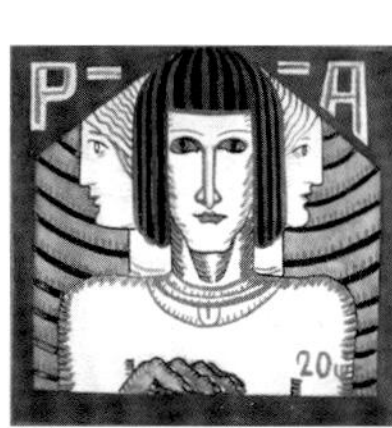

Design for Ra Cigarettes
Gouache on cardboard
3 2/5 x 4 3/5 in. (8.4 x 11.5 cm)
Signed: "Ivanova Liudmila Alexandrovna"
Dated: January 4, 1926
January 4, 1926
E4

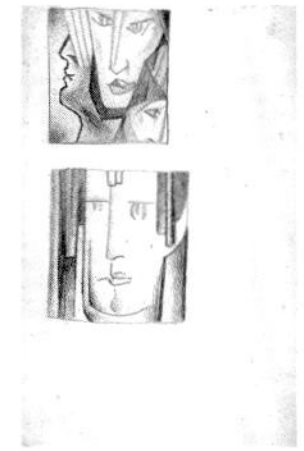

Geometricized Portraits in Two Squares
Pencil on paper
7 1/5 x 5 1/2 in. (18.0 x 13.7 cm)
c. 1930
C16

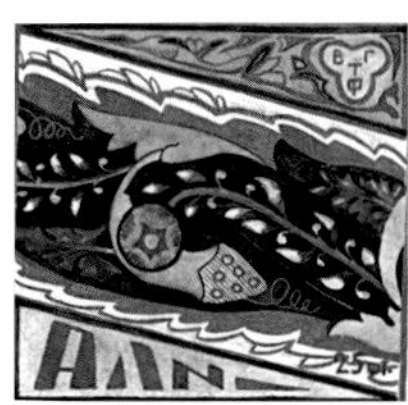

Floral Design for Ali Cigarettes
Gouache on cardboard
3 1/5 x 4 1/2 in. (8.0 x 8.3 cm)
Signed: "Ivanova Liudmila Alexandrovna"
1926
E5

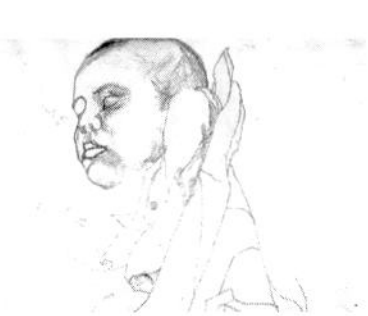

Sleeping Child (Son Vladimir?)
Pencil on cardboard
5 2/5 x 7 7/10 in. (13.3 x 19.3 cm)
1927
C20

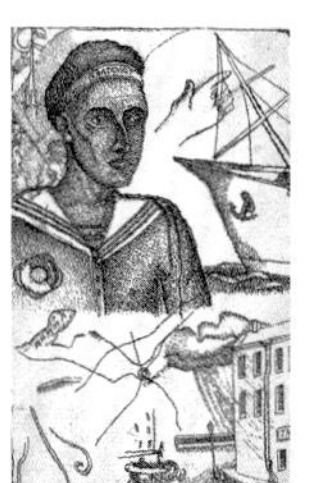

Blue Sailor
Ink on paper
5 2/5 x 3 1/2 in. (13.5 x 8.8 cm)
1927
C24

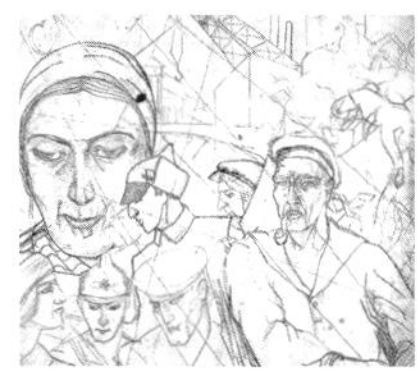

Urban Portraits with Woman and Sailor
Pencil on transparent paper
5 9/10 x 6 2/5 in. (14.7 x 16.1 cm)
1927
C25

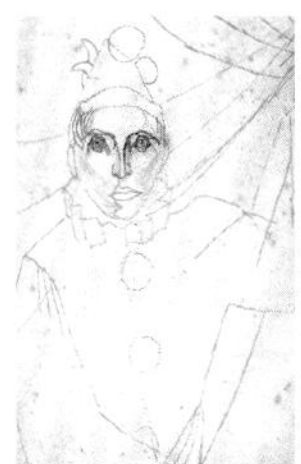

Clown
Pencil on cardboard
7 1/2 x 4 9/10 in. (18.7 x 12.3 cm)
1927
C29

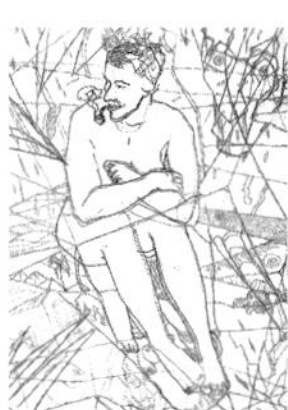

Woman Smoking a Pipe
Pencil on paper
11 2/5 x 8 4/5 in. (28.4 x 22.0 cm)
Verso: charcoal drawing of dog's snout
1926-1928
C32

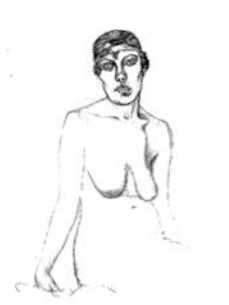

Seated Nude with Headband
Pencil on paper
14 x 10 1/5 in. (35.0 x 25.5 cm)
1928
C33

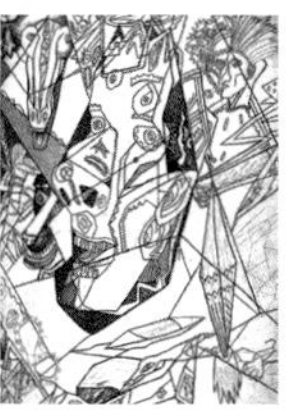

Head with Generic Native Imagery
Ink on paper
11 2/5 x 8 4/5 in. (28.6 x 22.0 cm)
1927-1930
C39

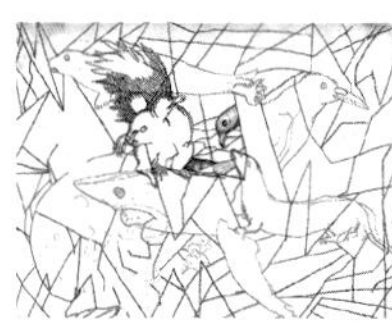

Animals with Geometric Motifs: Koala
Pencil and ink on paper
10 3/10 x 13 9/10 in. (25.7 x 34.7 cm)
1927-1930
C40

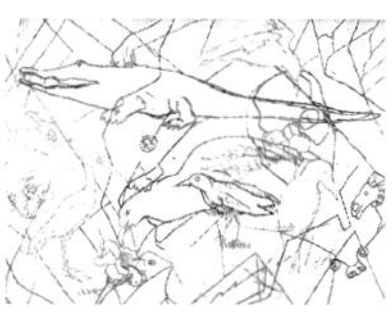

Animals with Geometric Motifs: Alligator
Pencil on paper
10 3/10 x 14 in. (25.6 x 34.9 cm)
1927-1930
C41

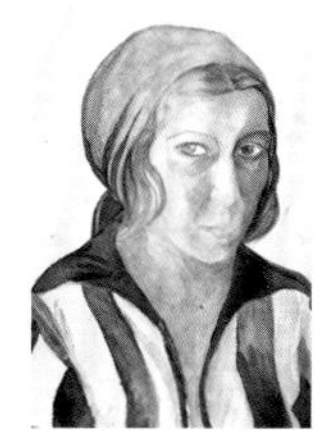

Woman in Red Kerchief: Right Three-Quarter View
Watercolor on paper
7 7/10 x 5 3/10 in. (19.2 x 13.3 cm)
Early 1930s
D8.1

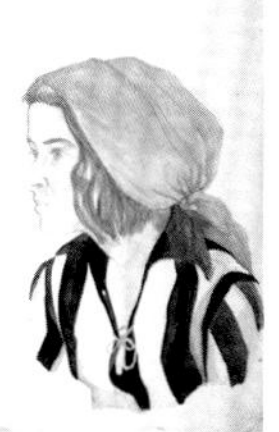

Woman in Red Kerchief: Left Three-Quarter View
Watercolor on paper
7 7/10 x 5 3/10 in. (19.3 x 13.3 cm)
Early 1930s
D8.5

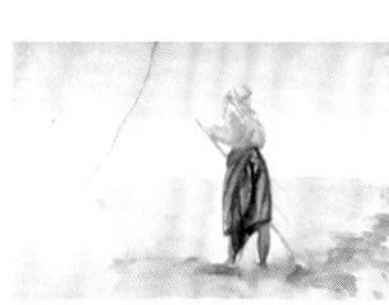

Peasant Girl Scything
Watercolor on paper
11 4/5 x 13 3/10 in. (29.6 x 33.3 cm)
1930s
D12

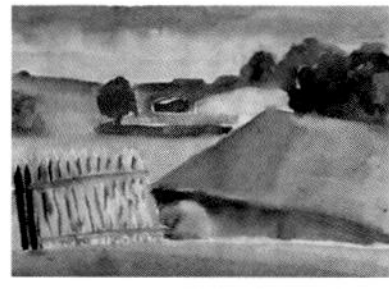

Rooftop and Picket Fence
Watercolor on paper
10 1/2 x 14 1/2 in. (26.2 x 36.2 cm)
Verso: Animal drawings
1930s
D13

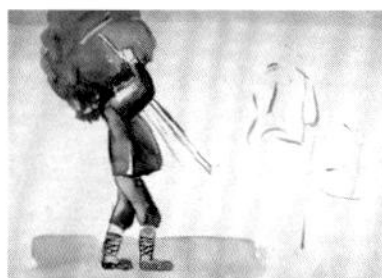

Peasant in Lapti
Watercolor on paper
10 1/2 x 14 3/5 in. (26.4 x 36.7 cm)
1930s
D14

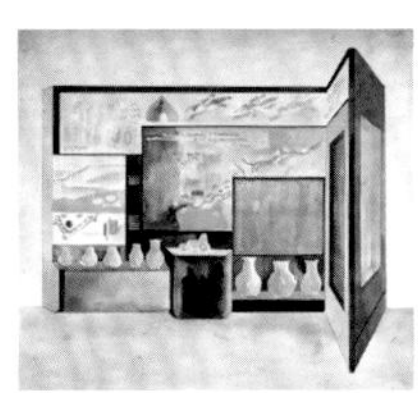

Design for Museum Exhibit
Pencil and watercolor on paper
14 3/10 x 15 1/10 in. (35.8 x 37.7 cm)
1931-1933
E6

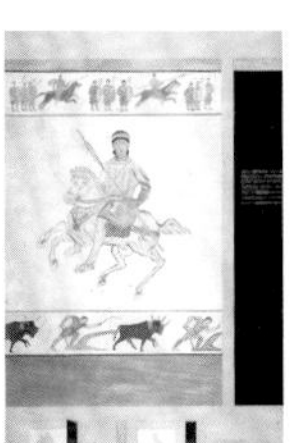

Exhibit Panel with Soldier on Horseback
Pencil and watercolor on paper
21 x 14.3 in. (52.4 x 35.8 cm)
Signed: "Ludm. Ivanova"
1931-1933
E7

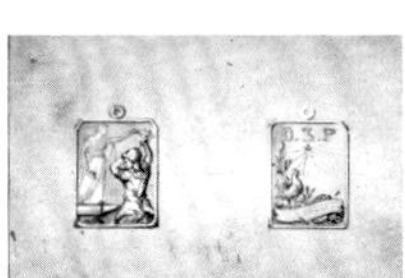

Design for Medals
Pencil on cardboard
3 4/5 x 5 1/5 in. (9.4 x 13.1 cm)
Late 1920s, early 1930s
E8

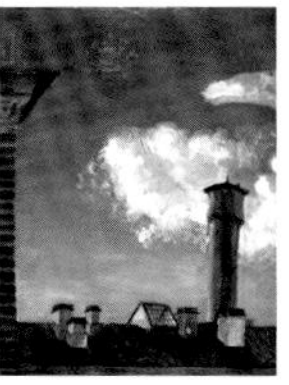

View of Rooftop Chimneys
Oil on canvas
12 3/10 x 9 7/10 in. (30.7 x 24.2 cm)
c. 1930
F43

Late Works (1934-1950)

Violet Huts Reflected on Water
Watercolor on paper
5 1/10 x 7 3/5 in. (12.7 x 18.9 cm)
Verso: Sketch of man and suitcase
Mid 1930s
D9

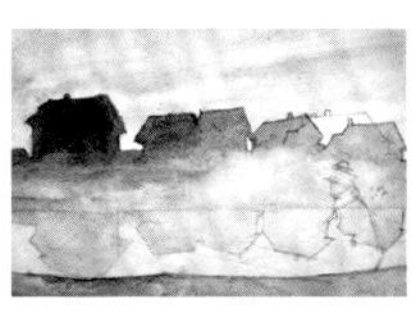

Church in Countryside
Oil on cardboard
9 3/8 x 15 3/4 in. (23.7 x 39.9 cm)
1934-1950
F1

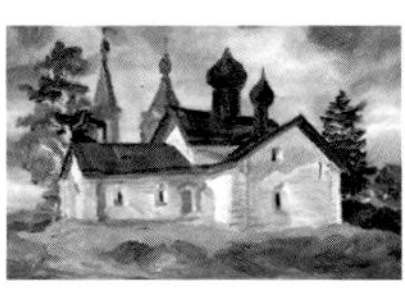

Single Tree with Purple Flowers
Oil on cardboard
9 1/2 x 15 1/2 in. (24.0 x 39.5 cm)
Inscription: "Dorogomu Vove v den' izozhdeniia
22/II/48g—Mama" ("To my dear Vova, on his
birthday, 2/22/48—Mama")
Verso: Stylized pencil sketch of country church
c. 1940s (before 1949)
F2

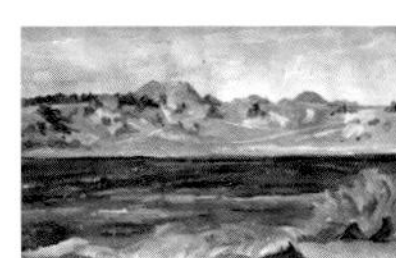

River in Hilly Landscape
Oil on cardboard
9 1/4 x 15 5/8 in. (23.5 x 39.5 cm)
c. 1940s (before 1949)
F3

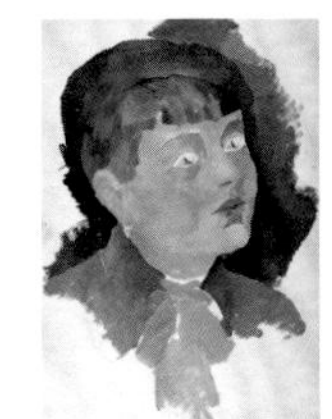

Young Woman with Beret and Scarf
Oil on cardboard
18 7/8 x 15 3/8 in. (48.0 x 39.0 cm)
Verso: Stamp identifies cardboard as having been
produced at the "Palette" Factory, Moscow, for the
use of students of oil painting, 26/11/41
After 1941
F4

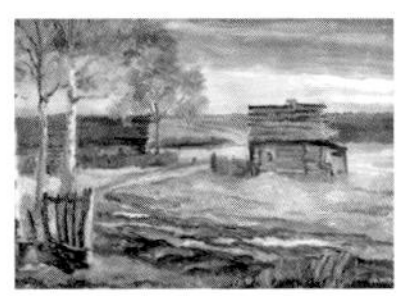

Curving Road with Figure in Red
Oil on cardboard
13 7/8 x 19 1/2 in. (35.3 x 49.5 cm)
Verso: Mathematical calculations in pen
1934-1950
F6

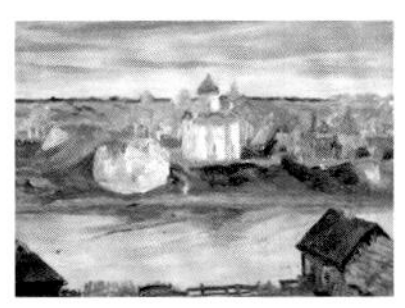

Church and Other Buildings on the Bank of a River
Oil on canvas
11 4/5 x 16 1/5 in. (29.4 x 40.5 cm)
1934-1950
F7

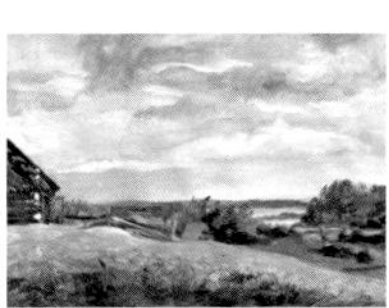

Edge of House on Green Slope
Oil on canvas
12 2/5 x 17 9/10 in. (31.0 x 44.8 cm)
1934-1950
F8

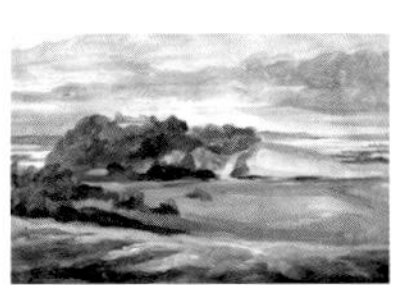

Landscape with Hill in Mid-Ground
Oil on canvas
12 2/5 x 17 9/10 in. (31.0 x 44.7 cm)
Late 1930s
F9

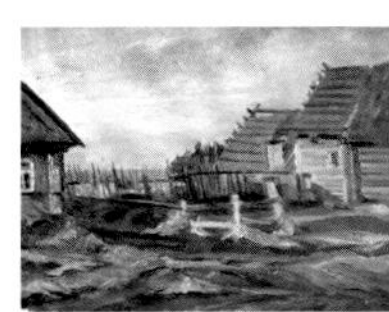

Orange Houses and Blue Fence
Oil on canvas
10 3/5 x 14 1/5 in. (26.7 x 35.4 cm)
1934-1950
F11

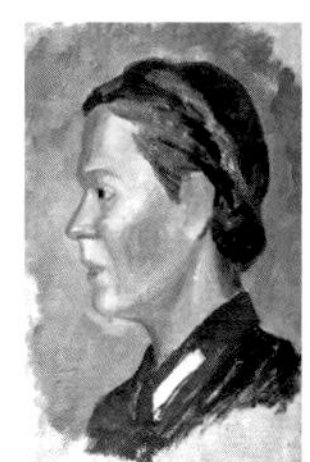

Profile of Woman in Green Uniform
Oil on canvas
16 13/16 x 11 in. (35.1 x 27.9 cm)
1934-1950
F13

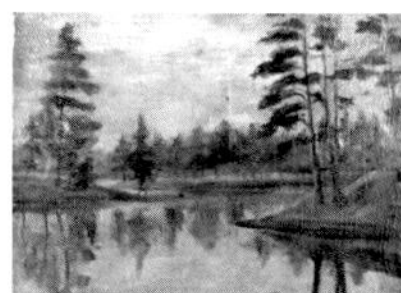

Lake at Dawn with Tall Evergreens
Oil on burlap
15 5/8 x 19 1/4 in. (39.7 x 48.9 cm)
1934-1950
F14

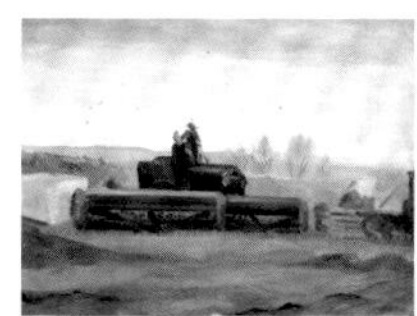

Farm Scene with Tractor
Oil on canvas
10 2/5 x 14 3/10 in. (25.9 x 35.8 cm)
Mid 1930s
F18

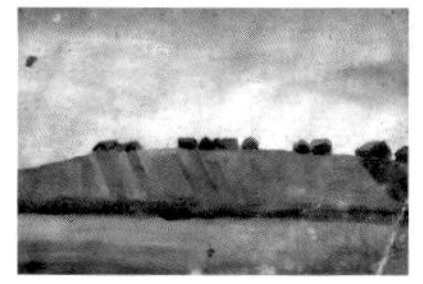

Violet Houses on Horizon
Oil on canvas
9 3/10 x 9 1/2 in. (23.3 x 23.7 cm)
Verso: Snow Covered Forest, oil on canvas,
Mid 1930s
F19a

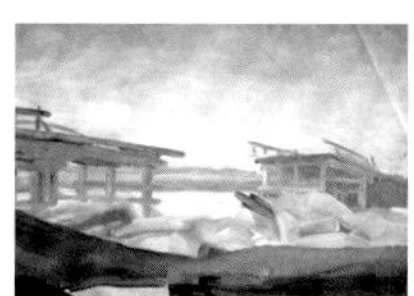

Broken Bridge During Thaw
Oil on canvas
10 1/5 x 14 3/10 in. (25.3 x 35.8 cm)
Mid 1930s
F21

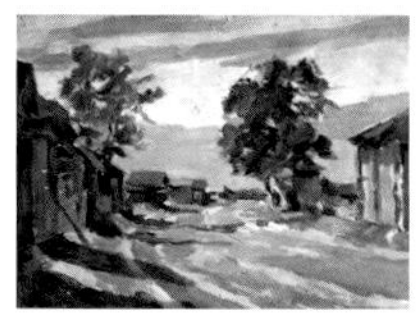

In the Village of Utekhina
Oil on paper
9 7/8 x 13 1/8 in. (25.0 x 33.3 cm)
Inscription: "B. Utekhina 42"
1942
F22

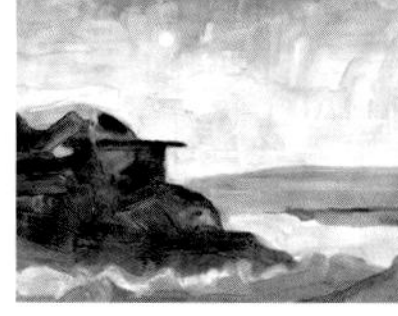

Muddy Riverbank with Northern Lights
Oil on canvas
10 7/8 x 12 5/8 in. (27.5 x 32.0 cm)
Mid 1930s
F23

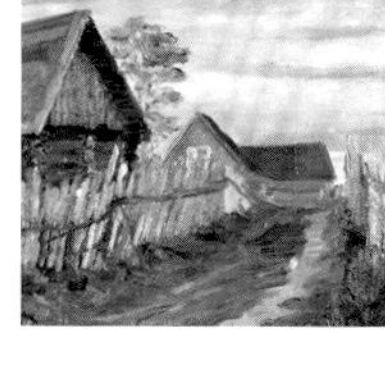

Houses Behind Fence at Roadside
Oil on canvas
10 3/8 x 11 1/2 in. (26.3 x 29.4 cm)
1934-1950
F24

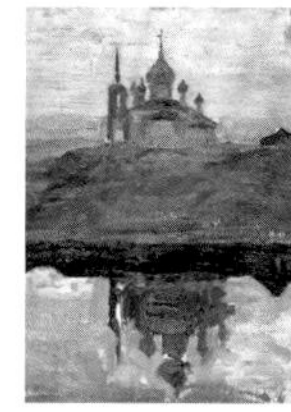

Church in Staraia Ladoga with Violet Reflection
Oil on canvas
13 3/5 x 10 2/5 in. (34.0 x 26.0 cm)
Signed and dated: "L. Ravdonikas 1948 Staraia
Ladoga" verso
1948
F27
Conservation supported by Ronald & Roxanne
Meyer

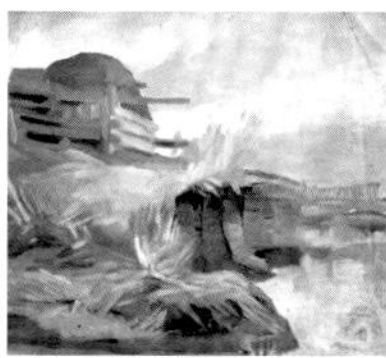

Fenced Haystack
Oil on canvas
9 7/8 x 11 3/8 in. (25.0 x 28.9 cm)
Mid 1930s
F29

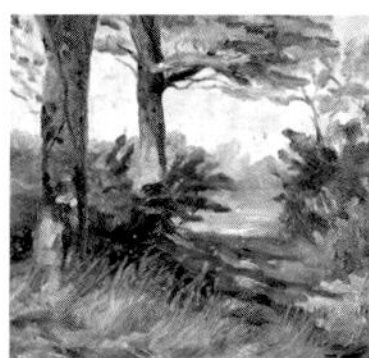

Spring Landscape
Oil on canvas
9 7/8 x 11 3/10 in. (25.0 x 28.2 cm)
1934-1950
F32

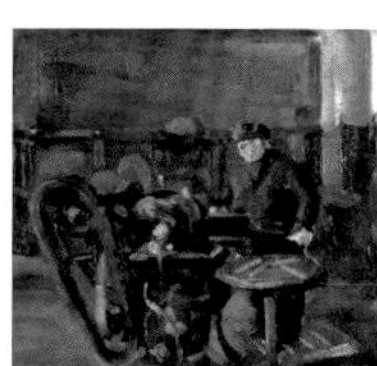

Worker in Factoryshop
Oil on canvas
10 5/8 x 12 1/8 in. (27.0 x 30.8 cm)
Late 1930s
F35

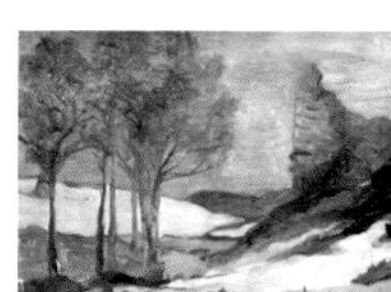

Winter Landscape with Trees
Oil on canvas
9 1/5 x 12 4/5 in. (23.0 x 32.0 cm)
1934-1950
F36

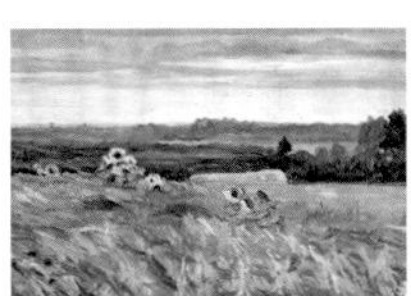

Summer Landscape with Sunflowers
Oil on canvas
10 1/5 x 15 2/5 in. (25.6 x 38.5cm)
1934-1950
F37

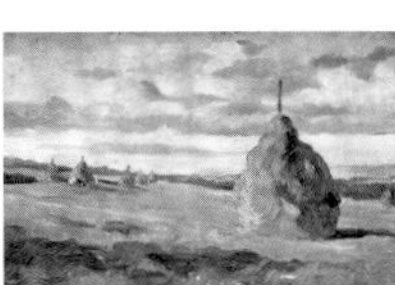

Summer Landscape with Haystacks
Oil on canvas
9 7/10 x 15 in. (24.2 x 37.6 cm)
1934-1950
F38

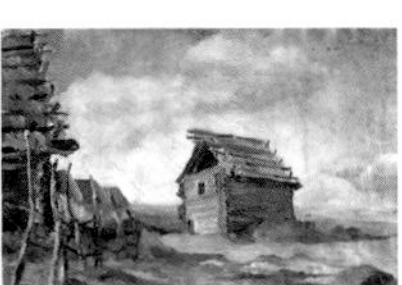

Huts, Fence and Landscape
Oil on canvas
10 x 15 1/10 in. (24.9 x 37.9 cm)
1934-1950
F40

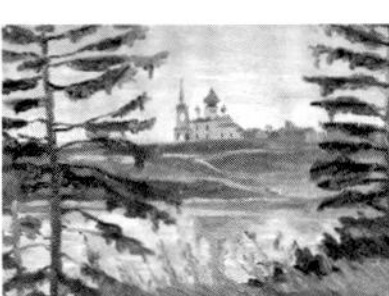

Church Framed by Two Fir Trees
Oil on canvas
10 7/10 x 15 1/5 in. (26.8 x 38.1 cm)
*Verso: Stamp of the All Union Cooperative of
Artists*
After 1933
F41

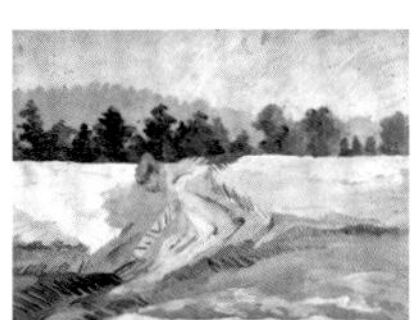

Path Through a Field
Oil on canvas
10 x 13 1/2 in. (24.9 x 33.8 cm)
Verso: Night, Crosses
Mid 1930s
F44

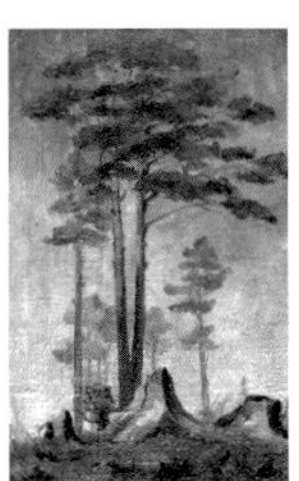

Stand of Tall Trees and Stumps
Oil on canvas
16 3/4 x 11 1/16 in. (42.5 x 29.5 cm)
1934-1950
F50

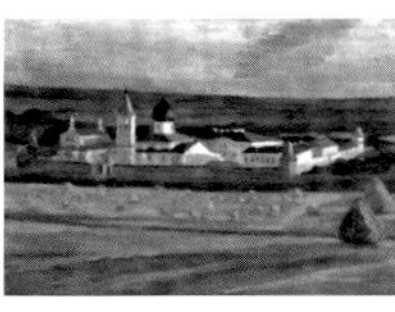

Monastery Complex
Oil on canvas
14 x 19 9/10 in. (34.9 x 49.8 cm)
1934-1950
F52

Archival Documents

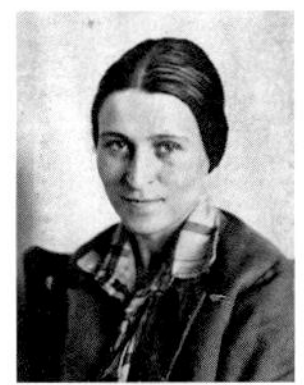

Photograph of Ivanova
2 1/5 x 1 7/10 in. (6.0 x 4.8 cm)
Dated: 1933
G1

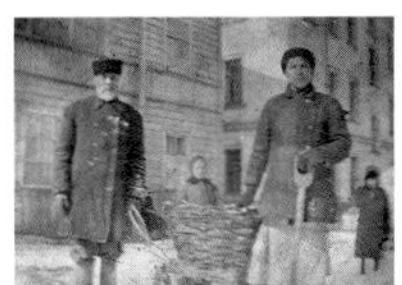

Photograph of Ivanova as a Child (Street Scene)
2 1/10 x 3 1/5 in. (5.8 x 8.7 cm)
c. 1910s
G2

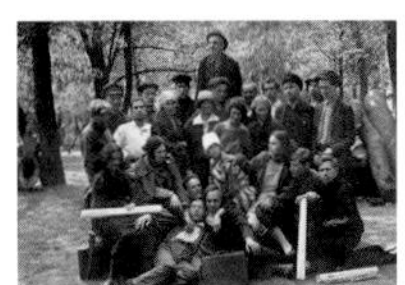

Photograph of Matiushin's Second Year Class
3 3/10 x 11 1/2 in. (9.0 x 31.0 cm)
Verso: Inscription of names
Dated: May 20th, 1925
G7

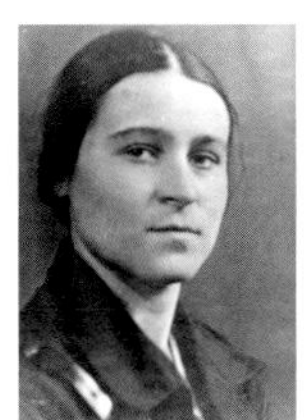

Photograph of Ivanova
6 1/2 x 4 1/5 in. (17.5 x 12.5 cm)
Dated: 1921
G8

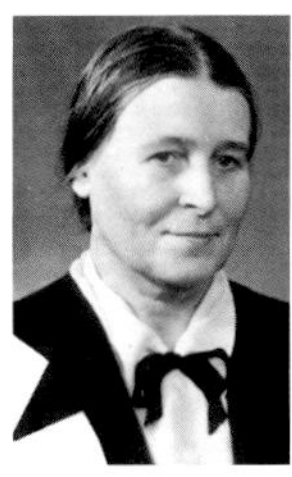

Photograph
1 9/10 x 1 1/2 in. (5.3 x 4.0 cm)
1955
G10

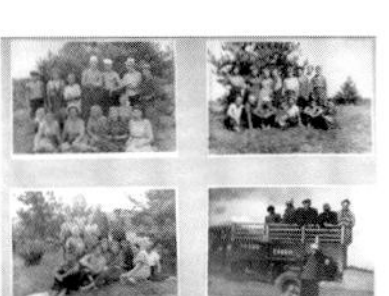

Four Photographs
4 3/10 x 6 1/2 in. (11.5 x 17.5 cm)
Individual photos
1940s
G13

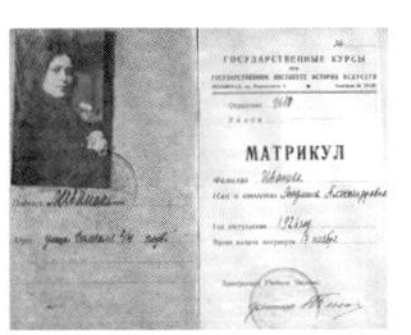

Photograph of Ivanova, Matrikula
6 7/10 x 7 3/5 in. (18.0 x 20.5 cm)
1926
G14

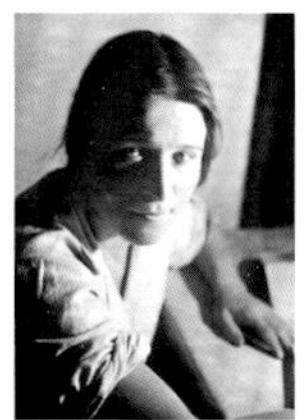

Photograph of Ivanova
4 3/10 x 3 1/10 in. (11.5 x 8.5 cm)
c. 1920s
G15

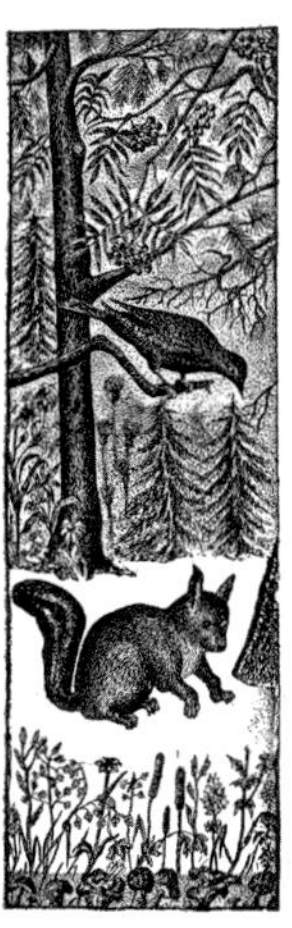

Illustration, page 39.
Wood engraving
9 4/5 x 7 1/5 in. (25.0 x 18.0 cm)
Kalevala: Finskii Narodnyi Epos (Kalevala:
A Finnish Folk Epic)
Ed. D. V. Bubrikha
Moscow, Leningrad: Academia, 1933

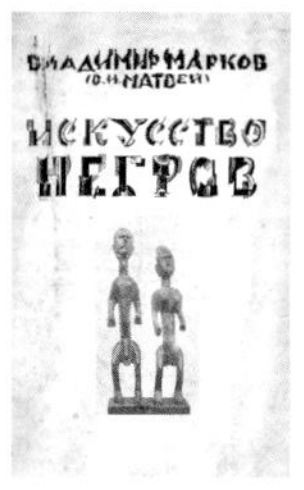

Vladimir Markov [Waldemars Matvejs pseud.]
Iskusstvo negrov (The Art of the Negroes).
Petrograd: NKP, 1919.
10 x 6 3/4 in. (25.2 x 17.0 cm)

V. Ravdonikas
Nasakalnye izobrazheniia Onezhskogo ozera
I Belogo moria (Cliff Drawings of Onezh Lake
and the White Sea)
Moscow, Leningrad: Academy of Arts of USSR
Vol. 1, 1936; Vol. 2, 1938
Collection of UC Berkeley Library